KU-111-725

REGENTS RENAISSANCE DRAMA SERIES

General Editor: Cyrus Hoy
Advisory Editor: G. E. Bentley

BARTHOLOMEW FAIR

BEN JONSON

Bartholomew Fair

Edited by

Edward B. Partridge

LONDON
EDWARD ARNOLD (PUBLISHERS) LTD.

Published in Great Britain by Edward Arnold (Publishers) Ltd.
First Published in Great Britain 1964

MANUFACTURED IN THE UNITED STATES OF AMERICA

Regents Renaissance Drama Series

The purpose of the Regents Renaissance Drama Series is to provide soundly edited texts, in modern spelling, of the more significant plays of the Elizabethan, Jacobean, and Caroline theater. Each text in the series is based on a fresh collation of all sixteenth- and seventeenth-century editions. The textual notes, which appear above the line at the bottom of each page, record all substantive departures from the edition used as the copy-text. Variant substantive readings among sixteenth- and seventeenth-century editions are listed there as well. In cases where two or more of the old editions present widely divergent readings, a list of substantive variants in editions through the seventeenth century is given in an appendix. Editions after 1700 are referred to in the textual notes only when an emendation originating in some one of them is received into the text. Variants of accidentals (spelling, punctuation, capitalization) are not recorded in the notes. Contracted forms of characters' names are silently expanded in speech prefixes and stage directions, and, in the case of speech prefixes, are regularized. Additions to the stage directions of the copy-text are enclosed in brackets. Stage directions such as "within" or "aside" are enclosed in parentheses when they occur in the copy-text.

Spelling has been modernized along consciously conservative lines. "Murther" has become "murder," and "burthen," "burden," but within the limits of a modernized text, and with the following exceptions, the linguistic quality of the original has been carefully preserved. The variety of contracted forms (*'em, 'am, 'm, 'um, 'hem*) used in the drama of the period for the pronoun *them* are here regularly given as *'em,* and the alternation between *a'th'* and *o'th'* (for *on* or *of the*) is regularly reproduced as *o'th'*. The copy-text distinction between preterite endings in *-d* and *-ed* is preserved except where the elision of *e* occurs in the penultimate syllable; in such cases, the final syllable is contracted. Thus, where the old editions read "threat'ned," those of the present series read "threaten'd." Where, in the old editions, a contracted preterite in *-y'd* would yield *-i'd* in modern spelling (as in "try'd," "cry'd," "deny'd"), the word is here given in its full form (e.g., "tried," "cried," "denied").

Punctuation has been brought into accord with modern practices. The effort here has been to achieve a balance between the generally light pointing of the old editions, and a system of punctuation which, without overloading the text with exclamation marks, semicolons, and dashes, will make the often loosely flowing verse (and prose) of the original syntactically intelligible to the modern reader. Dashes are regularly used only to indicate interrupted speeches, or shifts of address within a single speech.

Explanatory notes, chiefly concerned with glossing obsolete words and phrases, are printed below the textual notes at the bottom of each page. References to stage directions in the notes follow the admirable system of the Revels editions, whereby stage directions are keyed, decimally, to the line of the text before or after which they occur. Thus, a note on 0.2 has reference to the second line of the stage direction at the beginning of the scene in question. A note on 115.1 has reference to the first line of the stage direction following line 115 of the text of the relevant scene.

CYRUS HOY

Vanderbilt University

Contents

Abbreviations

Chambers	Sir Edmund Chambers. *The Elizabethan Stage*. Oxford, 1923.
Cotgrave	*A Dictionairie of the French and English Tongues.* London, 1611.
C.S.A.	*Bartholomew Fayre*. Ed. C. S. Alden. *Yale Studies in English*, XXV, 1904.
E.A.H.	*Bartholomew Fair*. Ed. E. A. Horsman. *The Revels Plays*. Cambridge, Mass., 1960.
F	*The Workes of Benjamin Jonson: The Second Volume*. London, 1640.
F_3	*The Works of Ben Jonson*. London, 1692.
G.	*The Works of Ben Jonson*. Ed. William Gifford. 9 vols. London, 1816. Revised by Francis Cunningham. London, 1875.
Grose	Francis Grose. *A Classical Dictionary of the Vulgar Tongue*. London, 1785.
H.S.	*Ben Jonson*. Ed. C. H. Herford, Percy and Evelyn Simpson. 11 vols. Oxford, 1925–1952.
J.	Ben Jonson:

A.	*The Alchemist,* 1610.
C.	*Catiline,* 1611.
D.A.	*The Diuell is an Asse,* 1616.
E.M.O.	*Every Man out of His Humor,* 1599.
Ep.	*Epigrammes.*
M.L.	*The Magnetick Lady,* 1632.
S.N.	*The Staple of Newes,* 1626.
V.	*Volpone,* 1605.

Markham	Gervase Markham. *Markhams Maister-peece . . . Containing all Knowledge belonging to a Smith, Farrier, or Horseleach*. 1610.

ABBREVIATIONS

Morley	Henry Morley. *Memoirs of Bartholomew Fair.* London, 1859.
Nares	Robert Nares. *A Glossary, or Collection of Words. . . .* Ed. J. O. Halliwell and Thomas Wright. 2 vols. London, 1882.
OED	*Oxford English Dictionary.*
S.D.	Stage direction.
Spencer	Hazelton Spencer, *Elizabethan Plays.* Boston, 1933.
S.P.	Speech prefix.
Stow	John Stow. *A Survey of London,* 1598, 1603. Ed. C. L. Kingsford. Oxford, 1908.
Stubbes	Phillip Stubbes. *The Anatomie of Abuses,* 1583. Ed. Furnivall (New Shakspere Soc., Series VI, Nos. 4, 6, 12). 1877–1882.
W.	*The Workes of Ben Jonson.* Ed. Peter Whalley. 7 vols. London, 1756.
1716	*The Workes of Ben Jonson.* 6 vols. London, 1716.

Introduction

> Bartholomew Faire begins on the twenty fourth day of *August*, and is then of so vast an extent that it is contained in no lesse then four several parishes, namely, Christ Church, Great and Little Saint Bartholomewes, and Saint Sepulchres. Hither resort people of all sorts, High and Low, Rich and Poore, from cities, townes, and countrys; of all sects, Papists, Atheists, Anabaptists, and Brownists: and of all conditions, good and bad, vertuous and vitious, Knaves and fooles, Cuckolds and Cuckoldmakers, Bauds, and Whores, Pimpes and Panders, Rogues and Rascalls, the little Loud-one and the witty wanton.

So begins *Bartholomew Faire, or Variety of fancies* . . . (1641), a quarto pamphlet which owes as much to Jonson's play as it does to the actual fair held in Smithfield. After its founding in 1120 by Rayer, Prior of St. Bartholomew's, the Fair gradually became a peculiar nexus of religion, trade, and pleasure. All three may have met most compatibly in the fifteenth century when miracle plays were given there, the Cloth Fair became dominant, and the pleasure itself had not become thoroughly coarsened. By 1539 the Fair was completely severed from the Church. By the seventeenth century, as both Jonson's play and the 1641 pamphlet make clear, it had become a haunt of pickpockets, roaring boys, and whores, and a spectacle noisy with the cries of hawkers, puppet masters, and magicians, and stinking with the sweat of the dog days of August and the smell of ale, roast pig, and gingerbread.

Representing the endless voracity of man for food and money and sensuous pleasure, the Fair offered at least two things that Jonson's imagination apparently needed in order to be released into comedy: a "Center attractive, to draw thither a diversity of Guests" and a full set of cheaters and cheated. Some of the cheaters used by Jonson are the bawds, cutpurses, and sly entrepreneurs native to the Fair. Others are Jonsonian creations like the frauds, Busy and Dame Purecraft, both of whom have grown rich by gulling brethren, or the respectable gentlemen, Quarlous and Winwife, each of whom acquires a rich wife by something less than scrupulous means. The cheated prove to be some of the finest fools ever to grace a stage. Cokes and the Littlewits generate the action by bringing the citizens and the gentry to the Fair—Cokes because he wants to romp around the booths, John Littlewit to see his puppet play produced, and Win to eat roast pig. With all the magnetism of a cheerful and willful child, Cokes draws along to the Fair his sister, Mrs. Overdo, his fiancée, Grace, and his tutor, Wasp; Winwife and Quarlous follow them more to enjoy Cokes's idiocy than the Fair's frivolity. The citizens of London—represented by the Littlewits, Dame Purecraft, and Zeal-of-the-Land Busy—seem scarcely more sophisticated than the gentry represented by Cokes, an Esquire of Harrow, and the gentle ladies, Grace Wellborn and Mrs. Overdo.

So much sounds like simple Jonsonian tactics: bring the gulls to be gulled. We might foresee that Edgworth, the cutpurse, aided by Nightingale, the ballad-singer, would steal both of Cokes's purses, and later the marriage license from Wasp so that Winwife, not Cokes, could marry Grace. Quarlous' similar success with Dame Purecraft; the comic jeopardy that the virtue of Win and Mrs. Overdo is put in by their witlessness; the watered ale; the decaying gingerbread; Ursula, the sweating, foul-mouthed pig-woman—all might be anticipated in this preposterous world. We see another of Jonson's extravagant caricatures of the social and economic system, though on a larger scale than ever before: "people of all sorts, High and Low, Rich and Poore, from cities, townes, and countrys"; and from all parts of England—Whit with his Irish brogue, Puppy, a Western man, and Nordern, a clothier from the North.

But the comic design is more complicated than a simple gulling of the gulls, as a synoptic view of the plot may indicate. In the first act the citizens, the country gentry, and the gentlemen of the town are assembled at the house of Littlewit. Only Justice Overdo is not presented until the second act, which he opens by announcing that he is going to discover and put down the enormities of the Fair. The rest of this act is given over to the folk of the Fair and to two sets of visitors. First, Quarlous and Winwife, the most sophisticated of the visitors, contemptuously view the booth of Ursula and quarrel with her. Second, Cokes and his entourage enter; after Cokes's small purse is stolen, Wasp, suspecting him, beats the innocent Overdo. The third act repeats the second with some remarkable parallels and differences. The third set of visitors, the Littlewits, Dame Purecraft, and Busy, enter. Once again, a purse of Cokes is stolen—the larger one this time. Once again, Overdo is suspected, but this time taken away under arrest. Just as the second act ends with the beating of Overdo, so the third ends with the arrest of Busy for having thrown over Joan Trash's gingerbread. Violence, gradually growing in the first three acts, explodes in the "vapors" of the fourth act. Here the contentiousness is most shrill. Cokes loses cloak, hat, and sword. Wasp, with irascible joy, enters into the game of vapors. Quarlous quarrels first with Winwife over Grace, then with Cutting over a circle on the ground. Punk Alice beats Mrs. Overdo because she thinks the rich ladies with their velvet haunches are taking her occupation away from her. The act ends with Wasp, Busy, and Overdo being put in the stocks, from which all soon escape. In the final act come the discoveries, most of which deflate. In the puppet show Busy is silenced by Dionysius. Quarlous gains a rich widow at the expense of Busy; Winwife, a lovely wife at the expense of Cokes. Overdo, like an *asinus ex cathedra,* reveals all that he has discovered about the others only to find himself humbled in turn by Quarlous and by his drunken wife. The comedy ends, as comedies about a Fair should, with a feast.

The plot is organized, then, to expose not merely the folly of the obviously foolish Cokes and Littlewits, but also the more harmful folly of the lawgivers—the "dry nurse," Wasp, the Puritan Busy with his loud braying of biblical phrases literally understood, and the magistrate Overdo with his philippics against ale and tobacco. The "careful fool" or the "serious ass," as Quarlous tells us when talking about Wasp, "takes pains to be one, and plays the fool, with the greatest diligence that can be." Grace claims that her guardian, Justice Overdo, is such a fool. Both she and Quarlous distinguish the careful from the careless fool like Cokes—innocent, unstudied, witless Cokes, one of nature's numbskulls. The careful fools are all figures of authority, and each is finally stripped of a large measure of his authority. Wasp is exposed as a master without self-mastery; Busy, a preacher without sense or sincerity; and Overdo, a judge without tolerance or judiciousness.

The judge and the preacher here represent two kinds of lawgivers especially prominent in Jacobean England—the Justice of the Peace and the Puritan. The constituted law is represented by such a collection of fools that one wonders why the criminals have not taken over even more of the Fair than they have. If Littlewit manages the causes of others in court as idiotically as he manages his own affairs outside, he must darken the counsels of even this opaque legal system. As for Quarlous, not enough of his Inns of Court training rubbed off on him to keep him from employing a pickpocket to steal a wedding license from Wasp. When His Majesty's Watch, Bristle and Haggis, put Wasp in the stocks, they are not awake enough to prevent his shifting in a hand for a foot—and so away. Then, in the midst of a scuffle with Trouble-All, the watchmen leave the other stocks open—and away go Busy and Overdo. Even the highest legal authority we meet, Justice Overdo, wishes to be thought only "a certain middling thing, between a fool and a madman" (II.ii.143). He succeeds. His folly is somewhat more serious than that of his constables; his madness is only less thorough than that of his ex-officer, Trouble-All, who has run so mad about the letter of the law that he will neither change his shirt nor urinate without a warrant from Overdo.

More savagely exposed are the other lawgivers, the Puritans. Busy is first described as being "fast by the teeth i' the cold turkey-pie, i' the cupboard, with a great white loaf on his left hand, and a glass of malmsey on his right" (I.vi.33–35). This vivid image of Busy's ravenous appetite prepares us for his later comic behavior at the Fair when he "scents" after the roast pig "like a hound" (III.ii.77.1.). He becomes most comic when he justifies his eating of pig by saying that it would be a public profession of his loathing of Judaism—a way of eating his pig and hating it too. The hypocrisy of the brethren appears not merely in the ease with which Busy makes the visit of Dame Purecraft and the Littlewits to the Fair "lawful," but also in the confession of Dame Purecraft that she has been like a female Volpone drawing "feasts and gifts from my entangled suitors," "a devourer, instead of a distributor of the alms," and a kind of ecclesiastically sanctioned bawd. Busy, as purely crafty as she, is an even more zealous engrosser of inheritances and lands, "the capital knave of the land" (V.ii.53–69). Jonson's (and his age's) principal objections to the Puritans are forcefully if unfairly represented in the actions of these precious two: hypocrisy, faction, superstitiousness, contentiousness, and contempt for classical antiquity or indeed for any learning other than that of scriptural revelation.

Overdo with his figures of rhetoric and his techniques of classical oratory burlesques the forum; Busy, Zeal-of-the-Land, with his biblical rhythms, his exhortations, and casuistical reasoning, burlesques the Puritan pulpit. One is a fool who perverts learning and blinds justice; the other is a knave who prizes only biblical law and curses all who seek light elsewhere. The Fair is judged by a Justice of the Peace (lately a scrivener, and new to the gentry) who is intolerant of all opposition and too intoxicated with his own office to discover the real enormities of England, and by a baker from Banbury whose fanaticism redoubles as his vision diminishes. Caught between the overdoer who is convinced that compassion is nearer a vice than a virtue, and a busybody who thinks ale a drink of Satan's (after he has drunk a pailful), and the puppet idols of Dagon, where could harmless folly and idle pleasure go? Where could wit and laughter and the theater go?

Bartholomew Fair finally answers these questions in the only way a play can: by being itself a work of art—foolish, witty, idle, joyful. As a play, it is another of Jonson's attempts to correct the extravagant humors and reconcile the contentious natures of men. In the Induction to one of his last plays, *The Magnetic Lady,* the Boy reviews Jonson's career as a long study of different humors or "manners of men" and describes the play to follow as "*Humors reconciled.*" To this, Probee, a choral character, says, "A bold undertaking! and farre greater, then the reconciliation of both Churches, the quarrel betweene humours having beene much the ancienter, and, in my poore opinion, the root of all Schisme, and Faction, both in Church and Commonwealth." Jonson's most ambitious attempt to reconcile the contentious humors of England and to defend even the most sensuous joy and even the lowest art from their Philistine detractors had been given to both the city and the court twenty years before. Its first performances by Lady Elizabeth's Men—at the Hope Theater on October 31, 1614, and, the next day, at court—were great successes. But no record of any other performance appears during the reigns of James I and Charles I, perhaps, in part, because of the rising power of the

Puritans. Later Lord Buckhurst thought that Busy finally silenced both the play and the stage which had silenced him.

> Many have been the vain attempts of wit
> Against the still prevailing hypocrit:
> Once, *and but once*, a poet got the day,
> And vanquished Busy in a puppet-play!
> But Busy rallying, filled with holy rage,
> Possessed the pulpit, and pulled down the stage.

In Lord Buckhurst's own age *Bartholomew Fair,* the second of Jonson's plays to be brought back to the Restoration stage, received the first of a number of productions on June 8, 1661. It was often performed up to 1731, when it apparently disappeared from the stage; only in the twentieth century has it been revived.

Modern criticism emphasizes, correctly, the good humor with which Jonson tries to reconcile the humors and the great art with which he defends art itself. The reconciliation is not easily or sentimentally reached. The Fair is pictured at its foulest, its whores in no way attractive, its rascals rarely kindhearted. In it pig-woman, horse-courser, and bawd feloniously merchandise unsound flesh. To it come fool, knave, hypocrite, and scoffer. Only time rescues both Win Littlewit and Mrs. Overdo from the prostitution which Whit, more eager to turn a penny than a head, had planned for them. But, while they save at least a semblance of virtue, Cokes loses everything at the Fair except his nitwitted delight in noise. Wasp is a fitting tutor for his brainless charge because there is, in his fixed and obsessive cantankerousness, something almost as childish as Cokes's prattle. The picture of egos pushing, chafing, knocking against each other, contending for place, power or just notice, has rarely been so vividly drawn as it is in this play in which the mere names of the characters express their contentious natures: Quarlous, Wasp, Busy, Overdo, Edgworth, Knockem, Ursula, Cutting, Bristle, Filcher, Sharkwell. And what a comic image of human striving is the endless bickering of the game of vapors or the puppet show in which both love and friendship explode into a nightmarish wrangle! If one can take life on the terms of the dirt and greed and idiocy of the Fair, one can take it on any terms.

Similarly, if one can take a play on the terms of the bathos and extravagance of the puppet show, one can take plays on any terms. Both life and the theater are rendered as mean as the comic spirit allows—too mean for some: even Pepys found the puppet show too profane and obscene. But, wanting no cheap victories, *Bartholomew Fair* prefers to risk a near defeat by sinking dangerously low for its paradigms of life and art.

Jonson prepares his listeners for both paradigms in the Induction. There we meet two theatrical functionaries. First, the Stagekeeper informs the audience that the author, disdaining his advice, has failed to hit the humors. His proof is that the play has no bullies, no jugglers with apes, no comedian like Tarlton with comic patter and rough-house fun. Contrasted with the vulgar taste of this Stagekeeper is the more artistic (and more pretentious) judgment of the Bookholder, who roundly dismisses the Stagekeeper and draws up, with the help of the Scrivener, a quasi-legal agreement with the audience. The articles of agreement are fundamental tenets in Jonson's dramatic criticism. The spectators are—or should properly be—hearers. (Jonson, always insistent on the primacy of words, emphasized listening the more popular the machines of Inigo Jones became.) These hearers are not all of a kind, some being curious and envious, the best being "favoring and judicious." All have the freedom to judge, since the author parted with his rights to the play when he gave it to be produced. The only provisos are that no one judge above his wit and that each depend on his own judgment, and not the judgment of others, whether acquired by contagion or trust or fashion. Furthermore, the author should be granted his *donnée*; he should not be censured for not having done what he never attempted. Nor should he be called scurrilous because his play uses decorously the language of low life. Aiming at types, not people, the play should not be thought of as a *comédie à clef*. Thus, even as his play begins, Jonson suggests the standards by which it ought to be judged.

But his chief defense of plays and of art in general comes in the puppet play, indirectly and ironically. Here he reveals how complex and esthetically interesting dramatic rendering of even a mean play can be. The range of possible esthetic reactions extends from those of the simple Cokes and the deluded Busy to that of the witty Leatherhead. Cokes seems so caught up in the dramatic world of the puppets that he acts as though the puppets were real. Before the play begins, he thinks that Leatherhead is jealous of his handling of the puppets. Then, as the play goes on, he comments on it and even interrupts it to ask the puppet master a question about the meaning of a speech. Most naive of all, he is worried about Leatherhead's being hurt when struck on the head by one of the puppets. If Cokes represents the simple-minded spectator, then Leatherhead represents the complex dramatic artist. Since he apparently manipulates the puppets (and perhaps speaks all their lines) as well as comments on them, he is both in the play as an actor and outside its central action as a chorus and still farther out when, as director, he answers Cokes. Wittily he tells Cokes, after one interruption, that the puppets Leander and Hero will be angry "if they hear you eavesdropping, now they are setting their match" (V.iv.292–293). At another point Leatherhead corrects the pronunciation of one of the puppets (in other words, either his own mispronunciation if he speaks all the parts or the mistake of one of his assistants); this puppet drops the illusion and answers him back. Leatherhead even burlesques the game of vapors when he has his puppets argue with him and start to beat him, at which moment he says, "Will ye murder me, masters both, i' mine own house?" (V.iv.232–253). Between the naive Cokes and the comic Leatherhead come Grace, Winwife, Knockem, and the others who watch the puppets and comment on Cokes and Busy. Observing all, even the observers, is, of course—the audience.

Leatherhead's wittiest moment is reached when he uses the puppet Dionysius to answer Busy, who takes—or pretends to take—the dramatic illusion for fact and who thinks the clothing of man in woman's garments a profanation. Dionysius gathers together in himself a number of the characters already presented: Wasp, as "the master of a school"; Overdo, as a tyrant of Syracuse; and the scrivener in the Induction, dressed, as he is, in a scrivener's furred gown. Since his name, too, links him with the god of the drama, Dionysius is logically the one to answer Busy's charge that a play is a profanation. Half the argument is won when Leatherhead, by setting his puppet to quarreling with Busy, makes the real person idiotic for humorlessly contending with an artificial creation. "What a desperate, profane wretch is this!" Winwife exclaims. "Is there any ignorance, or impudence, like his? To call his zeal to fill

him against a puppet?" (V.v.42–44). Since Leatherhead acts chorally in this scene to repeat the comments or the questions of Dionysius, he emphasizes how absurd a dispute between a man and a puppet is. Busy is finally refuted on specious grounds convincing only to one as fanatically blind as he is. To disprove that the puppet play is an abomination because the male puts on the apparel of the female, Dionysuis simply pulls up his garment to reveal that puppets are innocent because sexless. If Puritans have so little esthetic sense that they confuse fact and fiction, then they are justly refuted by the dubious argument that puppets, being sexless, cannot be accused of being impious in putting on female apparel. Busy failed to see, as another Johnson was to say, that the stage is only a stage, and the players only players. It has its own reality, its own truth, and its own laws: they are not those of the everyday world. The laws, the truth, the reality of the "real" world must not be used to silence the illusory world of the stage.

Larger than any of its themes is the play itself, its own best advocate. It may yield its magic slowly, almost reluctantly, at first sight repelling or at least keeping one off. But the longer one looks, the more richly one is rewarded. Finally, the world of the Fair comes pungently alive over these three hundred and fifty years, as any Jonson comedy does (if it does at all) largely through its strikingly sensuous diction, the individual syntax and rhythm of its speech, and the action which is rendered, at once naturalistic in detail and extravagant in effect. With a harsh music all its own *Bartholomew Fair* not merely ridicules man's eccentricities and castigates him for his follies, but also—uncommonly for Jonson—celebrates man's humanity and reconciles him to his limitations. At the end, after the most uncompromising of comic exposures, the least sentimental of saturnalia, and the most ironic of defenses of art and pleasure, each of us may be able to join all the fallen in saying, "I too am but Adam, flesh and blood."[1]

[1] The best single essay on *Bartholomew Fair* is by Jonas Barish in *Ben Jonson and the Language of Prose Comedy* (Cambridge, 1961), pp. 187–239. Good shorter essays appear in Volume II of the Herford and Simpson edition, and in Freda Townsend's *An Apologie for Bartholomew Fair: The Art of Ben Jonson's Comedies* (New York, 1947). Eugene M. Waith analyzes expertly the special staging problems of the play in "The Staging of *Bartholomew Fair*," *Studies in English Literature*, II (Spring, 1962), 181–195.

The Text

The only authoritative text for *Bartholomew Fair* is the folio printed in 1631 by John Beale for Robert Allot. This printing became part of the second volume of the 1640 folio by a tangled and still obscure process. After his paralytic stroke in 1628 Jonson began preparing to publish his unprinted plays and masques in a second volume to accompany the Folio of 1616. Among his unprinted plays was *Bartholomew Fair,* which, though originally produced in October, 1614, was not published in 1616. In 1631 a few copies of *Bartholomew Fair,* which with *The Devil is an Ass* and *The Staple of News* was printed by Beale, were distributed to friends and patrons of Jonson. Of these plays only *The Staple of News* was entered on the Stationer's Register by the publisher, Robert Allot. Perhaps because of Beale's bad printing Jonson abandoned the project. The unissued stock of the three plays was left on Allot's hands, where it remained until his death in 1635. In 1637 Allot's widow transferred her husband's rights to *Bartholomew Fair* and sixty other books to John Leggatt and Andrew Crooke. Richard Meighen, who may have bought up the sheets from Crooke, issued *Bartholomew Fair, The Devil is an Ass,* and *The Staple of News* with a title page, dated 1640, which described them as "The Second Volume of Jonson's Works." The other and greater portion of the Second Folio, consisting of the masques, the final plays, *The Underwood,* the translation of the *Ars Poetica,* and the prose works, was issued by Thomas Walkley early in 1641. These pieces published by Walkley were printed from Jonson's autograph papers left by him to Sir Kenelm Digby.

Because of the bad printing by Beale, Jonson's abandonment of the edition, and the publishing of the second volume after his death and without any corrections (so far as one can now tell), no one can rely on the text of the plays after 1616 with the assurance that even the most scrupulous can rely on the Folio of 1616. The mistakes made by Beale in the 1631–1640 text of the plays are varied and frequent: letters omitted; words dropped, misspelled, misspaced, printed twice over; sentences wrongly punctuated. The misprints in quires L and M of *Bartholomew Fair* are particularly bad.

The collation is A_1 recto (originally blank), Meighen's title page; A_1 verso, blank; A_2 recto, the title page; A_2 verso, blank; $A_{3\text{-}6}$, unpaged, the Prologue, the Persons of the Play, the Induction; B to M in fours, pages 1 to 88 (with pp. 12, 13, 31 misnumbered as 6, 3, 13, respectively), the text of the play and the Epilogue.

Though the Clarendon Press kindly granted to the University of Nebraska Press permission to modernize the text of the Herford and Simpson edition, the present text is not simply a modern spelling version of the Herford and Simpson text. Risking both a supererogation of virtue and the presumptuousness of doing over (and overdoing) what had been so magnificently done, the present editor has collated five copies of the play—two in the Folger Shakespeare Library, two in the Library of Congress, and one in the Newberry Library, Chicago. For the text as well as for the annotation, the Herford and Simpson edition and an excellent modern spelling edition by E. A. Horsman in the Revels Plays have proved invaluable.

Modernizing any Jonson play is dangerous because both the original spelling and the punctuation can be especially significant. Jonson often pointed his lines to indicate to actors the phrasing, the stress, and the pace of the lines. To change any of his careful punctuation is to risk distorting or losing the full Jonsonian effect; but not to modernize may be to make reading even more difficult than it normally is. Consequently, the punctuation and the spelling of the Folio have been modernized, but cautiously. The Folio stage directions have been kept; additions to them (usually from Gifford's edition) have been enclosed in brackets.

BARTHOLOMEW FAIR

THE PROLOGUE TO THE KING'S MAJESTY.

Your Majesty is welcome to a Fair;
Such place, such men, such language and such ware,
You must expect: with these, the zealous noise
Of your land's Faction, scandaliz'd at toys,
As babies, hobbyhorses, puppet-plays,
And such like rage, whereof the petulant ways
Yourself have known, and have been vex'd with long.
These for your sport, without particular wrong
Or just complaint of any private man
(Who of himself or shall think well or can),
The Maker doth present: and hopes tonight
To give you for a fairing, true delight.

PROLOGUE] for the performance at court, November 1, 1614.
4. *Faction*] the Puritans.
4. *toys*] trifles, rubbish.
5. *babies*] dolls.
12. *fairing*] a present bought at a fair.

THE PERSONS OF THE PLAY

JOHN LITTLEWIT	*A Proctor*
SOLOMON	*His man*
WIN LITTLEWIT	*His wife*
DAME PURECRAFT	*Her mother, and a widow*
ZEAL-OF-THE-LAND BUSY	*Her suitor, a Banbury man*
WINWIFE	*His rival, a gentleman*
QUARLOUS	*His companion, a gamester*
BARTHOLOMEW COKES	*An Esquire of Harrow*
HUMPHREY WASP	*His man*
ADAM OVERDO	*A Justice of Peace*
DAME OVERDO	*His wife*
GRACE WELLBORN	*His ward*
LANTERN LEATHERHEAD	*A Hobbyhorse-seller*
JOAN TRASH	*A Gingerbread-woman*
EZEKIEL EDGWORTH	*A Cutpurse*
NIGHTINGALE	*A Ballad-singer*
URSULA	*A Pig-woman*
MOONCALF	*Her Tapster*
JORDAN KNOCKEM	*A Horse-courser, and Ranger o' Turnbull*
VAL CUTTING	*A Roarer*
CAPTAIN WHIT	*A Bawd*

2. Solomon] *not in F; G. first listed the names of most of the minor characters, such as* Haggis, Bristle, Filcher, Puppy, Nordern.

---

1. *Proctor*] agent or attorney.

5. *Banbury*] town in Oxfordshire noted for its zealous Puritans and for its cakes.

7. Quarlous] contentious.

7. *gamester*] rake (cf. *game*, l. 23; prostitution).

8. Cokes] proverbial name for a fool.

18. Mooncalf] misshapen from birth because born under malignant influence of the moon.

19. *Horse-courser*] dealer in horses already ridden.

19. *Ranger*] 1. keeper of a park; 2. rake.

20. *Turnbull*] prostitute's haunt in Clerkenwell.

21. Cutting] a "cutter," bully or "roarer."

PUNK ALICE — *Mistress o' the game*
TROUBLE-ALL — *A madman*
HAGGIS, BRISTLE — *Watchmen*
POCHER — *A Beadle*
FILCHER, SHARKWELL — *Doorkeepers*
PUPPY — *A Wrestler*
NORDERN — *A Clothier*
MOUSETRAP MAN (Later called TINDERBOX-MAN)
Costermonger
Corncutter
Passengers
Puppets

34. *Corncutter*] *G.; not in F.* 35. *Passengers*] *G.;* Porters *F.*

---

23. Punk] whore.
29. Sharkwell] "shark," swindle.
33. *Costermonger*] seller of costards (apples).

THE INDUCTION ON THE STAGE.

[*ENTER*] STAGE-KEEPER.

STAGE-KEEPER.

Gentlemen, have a little patience, they are e'en upon coming, instantly. He that should begin the play, Master Littlewit, the Proctor, has a stitch new fall'n in his black silk stocking; 'twill be drawn up ere you can tell twenty. He plays one o' the Arches, that dwells about the Hospital, and he has a very pretty part. But for the whole play, will you ha' the truth on't? (I am looking, lest the poet hear me, or his man, Master Brome, behind the arras) it is like to be a very conceited scurvy one, in plain English. When't comes to the Fair once, you were e'en as good go to Virginia for anything there is of Smithfield. He has not hit the humors, he does not know 'em; he has not convers'd with the Bartholomew-birds, as they say; he has ne'er a sword and buckler man in his Fair, nor a little Davy, to take toll o' the bawds there, as in my time, nor a Kindheart, if anybody's teeth should chance to ache in his play. Nor a juggler with a well-educated ape to come over the chain, for the King of England, and back again for the Prince, and sit still on his arse for the Pope, and the King of Spain! None o' these fine sights! Nor has he the canvas-cut i' the night, for a hobbyhorse-man to creep in to his she-neighbor, and take his leap there! Nothing! No,

---

5. *Arches*] Court of Arches in Bow Church, court of appeal from the diocesan courts.

8. *Brome*] Richard Brome, servant, friend and, as playwright, imitator of Jonson.

9. *arras*] hanging tapestry.

9. *conceited*] fantastic.

11. *Smithfield*] site of the Fair, just to the north of Moorfields, outside the old city of London.

12. *humors*] odd behavior.

14. *sword and buckler man*] ruffian reputedly expert with weapons.

14–15. *little Davy*] a notorious bully.

16. *Kindheart*] an itinerant tooth-drawer.

and some writer (that I know) had had but the penning o' this matter, he would ha' made you such a jig-a-jog i' the booths, you should ha' thought an earthquake had been i' the Fair! But these master-poets, they will ha' their own absurd courses; they will be inform'd of nothing! He has, sir-reverence, kick'd me three or four times about the Tiring-house, I thank him, for but offering to put in, with my experience. I'll be judg'd by you, gentlemen, now, but for one conceit of mine! Would not a fine pump upon the stage ha' done well, for a property now? And a punk set under upon her head, with her stern upward, and ha' been sous'd by my witty young masters o' the Inns o' Court? What think you o' this for a show, now? He will not hear o' this! I am an ass! I! and yet I kept the stage in Master Tarlton's time, I thank my stars. Ho! and that man had liv'd to have play'd in *Bartholomew Fair,* you should ha' seen him ha' come in, and ha' been cozened i' the cloth-quarter, so finely! And Adams, the rogue, ha' leap'd and caper'd upon him, and ha' dealt his vermin about, as though they had cost him nothing. And then a substantial watch to ha' stol'n in upon 'em, and taken 'em away, with mistaking words, as the fashion is, in the stage-practice.

[*Enter*] Book-holder, Scrivener, *to him.*

BOOK-HOLDER.

How now? what rare discourse are you fall'n upon? ha! Ha' you found any familiars here, that you are so free?

---

28. *sir-reverence*] with apologies (altered from "save-reverence").
29–30. *to put in*] to intervene or get in (a word).
35. *Inns o' Court*] houses of law students: Lincoln's Inn, the Inner Temple, the Middle Temple, Gray's Inn.
37. *Tarlton*] principal comedian of the Queen's Men until his death in 1588.
40. *cloth-quarter*] a line of booths along the north wall of St. Bartholomew's Church; also an allusion to one of Tarlton's jests, which relates how a "coney catcher" stole his clothes.
40. *Adams*] a fellow actor in the Queen's company.
42. *vermin*] fleas? (C.S.A.)
45.1 Book-holder] prompter.

What's the business?

STAGE-KEEPER.

Nothing, but the understanding gentlemen o' the ground here ask'd my judgment.

BOOK-HOLDER.

Your judgment, rascal? For what? Sweeping the stage? Or gathering up the broken apples for the bears within? Away rogue, it's come to a fine degree in these spectacles when such a youth as you pretend to a judgment.

[*Exit* Stage-keeper]

And yet he may, i' the most o' this matter i' faith: for the author hath writ it just to his meridian, and the scale of the grounded judgments here, his play-fellows in wit. Gentlemen; not for want of a prologue, but by way of a new one, I am sent out to you here, with a scrivener, and certain articles drawn out in haste between our author, and you; which if you please to hear, and as they appear reasonable, to approve of, the play will follow presently. Read, scribe, gi' me the counterpane.

SCRIVENER.

Articles of Agreement, indented, between the spectators or hearers, at the Hope on the Bankside, in the County of Surrey, on the one party; and the author of *Bartholomew Fair* in the said place and county, on the other party: the one and thirtieth day of October, 1614, and in the twelfth year of the reign of our Sovereign Lord, James, by the grace of God King of England, France, and Ireland; Defender of the Faith; and of Scotland the seven and fortieth.

INPRIMIS, It is covenanted and agreed, by and between the parties above-said, and the said spectators, and hearers, as well the curious and envious, as the favoring and judicious, as also the grounded judgments and under-

49. *understanding*] punning reference to the spectators standing in the pit.

52. *bears*] in the Hope Theatre the stage was placed on trestles which were removed for bear-baiting.

56. *meridian*] fullest extent of the stage-keeper's faculties.

63. *counterpane*] opposite part of an indenture.

standings, do for themselves severally covenant and agree, to remain in the places their money or friends have put them in, with patience, for the space of two hours and an half, and somewhat more. In which time the author promiseth to present them, by us, with a new sufficient play called *Bartholomew Fair,* merry, and as full of noise as sport: made to delight all, and to offend none; provided they have either the wit or the honesty to think well of themselves.

It is further agreed that every person here have his or their free-will of censure, to like or dislike at their own charge, the author having now departed with his right: it shall be lawful for any man to judge his six pen'orth, his twelve pen'orth, so to his eighteenpence, two shillings, half a crown, to the value of his place: provided always his place get not above his wit. And if he pay for half a dozen, he may censure for all them too, so that he will undertake that they shall be silent. He shall put in for censures here, as they do for lots at the lottery: marry, if he drop but sixpence at the door, and will censure a crown's worth, it is thought there is no conscience, or justice in that.

It is also agreed, that every man here exercise his own judgment, and not censure by contagion, or upon trust, from another's voice, or face, that sits by him, be he never so first in the commission of wit: as also, that he be fix'd and settled in his censure, that what he approves, or not approves, today, he will do the same tomorrow, and if tomorrow, the next day, and so the next week (if need be): and not to be brought about by any that sits on the

---

87. *censure*] judgment.

89–91. *six pen'orth . . . crown*] references to prices of seats in the Jacobean theater; exceptionally high, perhaps because, as Chambers suggests (II, 534) "a new play at a new house."

95. *lottery*] a lottery, apparently opened in 1612 under royal patronage, for furthering the plantation of colonies in Virginia.

100. *contagion*] corrupting contact.

102. *commission of wit*] body of critics; a commission is a body authorized to conduct an investigation.

bench with him, though they indict and arraign plays daily. He that will swear *Jeronimo* or *Andronicus* are the best plays yet, shall pass unexcepted at, here, as a man whose judgment shows it is constant, and hath stood still, these five and twenty, or thirty, years. Though it be an ignorance, it is a virtuous and staid ignorance; and next to truth, a confirm'd error does well; such a one the author knows where to find him.

It is further covenanted, concluded and agreed, that how great soever the expectation be, no person here is to expect more than he knows, or better ware than a Fair will afford: neither to look back to the sword-and-buckler age of Smithfield, but content himself with the present. Instead of a little Davy, to take toll o' the bawds, the author doth promise a strutting Horse-courser, with a leer Drunkard, two or three to attend him, in as good equipage as you would wish. And then for Kindheart, the tooth-drawer, a fine oily Pig-woman with her Tapster to bid you welcome, and a consort of Roarers for music. A wise Justice of Peace *meditant,* instead of a juggler with an ape. A civil cutpurse *searchant.* A sweet Singer of new Ballads *allurant*: and as fresh an Hypocrite as ever was broach'd *rampant.* If there be never a Servant-monster i' the Fair, who can help it? he says; nor a nest of antics? He is loth to make Nature afraid in his plays, like those that beget *Tales, Tempests,* and such like drolleries,

---

107. *bench*] refers to both the law court and the seats on the stage sometimes occupied by "grave wits" (cf. *S.N.*, Induction, ll. 16–21).

108. *Jeronimo . . . Andronicus*] Kyd's *Spanish Tragedy* and Shakespeare's *Titus Andronicus.*

122. *leer*] looking askance; sly.

123. *equipage*] retinue; dress.

129–132. *Servant-monster . . . Tempests*] Caliban is called "servant-monster" three times in *The Tempest,* III.iii; the "nest of antics" may allude to the dance of satyrs in *The Winter's Tale,* IV.iv.334; elsewhere Jonson criticized the *"Concupiscence of Daunces, and Antickes"* (Preface to *A.*) and the "Iig-given times" (dedication of *C.*).

130. *nest*] group.

131. *antics*] originally, grotesques in art; here clowns or clownish dances.

132. *drolleries*] comic entertainments.

to mix his head with other men's heels; let the concupiscence of jigs and dances reign as strong as it will amongst you: yet if the puppets will please anybody, they shall be entreated to come in.

In consideration of which, it is finally agreed by the foresaid hearers and spectators that they neither in themselves conceal, nor suffer by them to be concealed, any state-decipherer, or politic picklock of the scene, so solemnly ridiculous as to search out who was meant by the Gingerbread-woman, who by the Hobbyhorse-man, who by the Costermonger, nay, who by their wares; or that will pretend to affirm, on his own inspired ignorance, what Mirror of Magistrates is meant by the Justice, what great lady by the Pig-woman, what conceal'd statesman by the Seller of Mousetraps, and so of the rest. But that such person, or persons so found, be left discovered to the mercy of the author, as a forfeiture to the stage, and your laughter, aforesaid; as also, such as shall so desperately, or ambitiously, play the fool by his place aforesaid, to challenge the author of scurrility because the language somewhere savors of Smithfield, the booth, and the pig-broth, or of profaneness because a madman cries, "God quit you," or "bless you." In witness whereof, as you have preposterously put to your seals already (which is your money), you will now add the other part of suffrage, your hands. The play shall presently begin. And though the Fair be not kept in the same region that some here, perhaps, would have it, yet think that therein the author

---

140. *politic*] shrewd.

140. *picklock*] c.f. *M.L.*, II, Chorus, 11–14: "It is picking the Lock of the Scene; not by opening it the faire way with a Key. A *Play*, though it apparell, and present vices in generall, flies from all particularities in persons."

145. *Mirror of Magistrates*] at once an echo of Whetstone's *Mirour for Magestrates of Cyties* (1584), in which a magistrate was advised to disguise himself and frequent places of entertainment to discover their real character, and a warning against identifying Overdo with Sir Thomas Hayes, Lord Mayor of London in 1614, who used this comic method of uncovering abuses (cf. H.S. X, 177).

152. *challenge*] accuse.

156. *preposterously*] in reversed order.

157. *suffrage*] approval.

hath observ'd a special decorum, the place being as dirty as Smithfield, and as stinking every whit.

Howsoever, he prays you to believe his ware is still the same, else you will make him justly suspect that he that is so loth to look on a baby, or an hobbyhorse, here, would be glad to take up a commodity of them, at any laughter, or loss, in another place. [*Exeunt.*]

---

161. *decorum*] fitness.
166. *commodity*] quantity.

Bartholomew Fair

[I.i] [*Enter*] Littlewit.

LITTLEWIT.

A pretty conceit, and worth the finding! I ha' such luck to spin out these fine things still, and like a silkworm, out of myself. Here's Master Bartholomew Cokes, of Harrow o' th' Hill, i' th' county of Middlesex, esquire, takes forth his license to marry Mistress Grace Wellborn of the said place and county: and when does he take it forth? Today! The four and twentieth of August! Bartholomew day! Bartholomew upon Bartholomew! There's the device! Who would have mark'd such a leap-frog chance now? A very less than ames-ace, on two dice! Well, go thy ways, John Littlewit, Proctor John Littlewit: one o' the pretty wits o' Paul's, the Littlewit of London (so thou art call'd) and something beside. When a quirk, or a quiblin does 'scape thee, and thou dost not watch, and apprehend it, and bring it afore the constable of conceit (there now, I speak quib too), let 'em carry thee out o' the archdeacon's court into his kitchen, and make a Jack of thee, instead of a John. (There I am again, la!)

[*Enter*] *to him* Win.

---

8. *device*] ingenious contrivance.

9. *leap-frog chance*] one in which it does not matter which is uppermost.

10. *ames-ace*] double ace (*ambas as*), the lowest possible throw with two dice.

12. *Paul's*] St. Paul's Church, whose middle aisle was a fashionable meeting place in Jacobean London.

13. *quirk*] quip.

13. *quiblin*] quibble, pun.

15. *conceit*] wit.

17. *Jack*] laborer; knave.

Win, good morrow, Win. Aye marry, Win! Now you look finely indeed, Win! This cap does convince! You'd not ha' worn it, Win, nor ha' had it velvet, but a rough country beaver, with a copper-band, like the coney-skin woman of Budge-row? Sweet Win, let me kiss it! And her fine high shoes, like the Spanish lady! Good Win, go a little, I would fain see thee pace, pretty Win! By this fine cap, I could never leave kissing on't.

WIN.

Come, indeed la, you are such a fool, still!

LITTLEWIT.

No, but half a one, Win, you are the tother half: man and wife make one fool, Win. (Good!) Is there the proctor, or doctor indeed, i' the diocese, that ever had the fortune to win him such a Win! (There I am again!) I do feel conceits coming upon me, more than I am able to turn tongue to. A pox o' these pretenders to wit, your Three Cranes, Mitre and Mermaid men! Not a corn of true salt, nor a grain of right mustard amongst them all. They may stand for places or so, again' the next witfall, and pay twopence in a quart more for their canary than other men. But gi' me the man can start up a justice of wit out of six-shillings beer, and give the law to all the poets, and poet-suckers, i' town, because they are the players' gossips! 'Slid, other men have wives as fine as the players, and as well dress'd. Come hither, Win.

---

20. *convince*] overcome.

22. *beaver*] a hat of beaver's fur.

23. *Budge-row*] where "Budge-Furre" (lamb skin with the wool turned outward) was sold (cf. Stow, I, 250).

24. *the Spanish lady*] In *D.A.* the Spanish dress of an English widow is said to be all the rage (II.viii.25–29; III.iv.13).

34. *Three Cranes, Mitre . . . Mermaid*] popular taverns in Jacobean London; Beaumont's *Letter to Ben Johnson* and Keats's *Lines on Mermaid Tavern* celebrate the wit combats at the Mermaid.

34. *corn*] grain.

36. *again'*] against; in anticipation of.

37. *canary*] a sweet wine made on the Canary Islands.

39. *six-shillings beer*] small beer sold at 6*s*. a barrel.

40. *poet-suckers*] sucking (that is, immature) poets.

41. *gossips*] friends.

[I.ii] [*Enter to them*] Winwife.

WINWIFE.

Why, how now, Master Littlewit! Measuring of lips or molding of kisses? Which is it?

LITTLEWIT.

Troth, I am a little taken with my Win's dressing here! Does't not fine, Master Winwife? How do you apprehend, sir? She would not ha' worn this habit. I challenge all Cheapside to show such another—Moorfields, Pimlico path, or the Exchange, in a summer evening—with a lace to boot, as this has. Dear Win, let Master Winwife kiss you. He comes a-wooing to our mother, Win, and may be our father perhaps, Win. There's no harm in him, Win.

WINWIFE.

None i' the earth, Master Littlewit.

LITTLEWIT.

I envy no man my delicates, sir.

WINWIFE.

Alas, you ha' the garden where they grow still! A wife here with a strawberry breath, cherry lips, apricot cheeks, and a soft velvet head, like a melicotton.

LITTLEWIT.

Good i' faith! Now dullness upon me, that I had not that before him, that I should not light on't as well as he! Velvet head!

WINWIFE.

But my taste, Master Littlewit, tends to fruit of a later kind: the sober matron, your wife's mother.

---

4. *apprehend*] think.

6. *Cheapside*] "Mercers, and Haberdashers vsed to keepe their shoppes in West Cheape" (Stow, I, 81).

6. *Moorfields*] ten acres of marsh outside the City wall in Moorfields and Finsbury were reclaimed in 1606 and made into a park.

6. *Pimlico*] a Hoxton house noted for cakes and ale.

7. *Exchange*] the New Exchange in the Strand, built in 1608–1609; a fashionable resort for ladies.

7. *lace*] stripe.

8. *to boot*] in addition.

12. *delicates*] delights.

15. *melicotton*] a peach grafted on a quince.

LITTLEWIT.

Aye! We know you are a suitor, sir. Win and I both wish you well: by this license here, would you had her, that your two names were as fast in it, as here are a couple. Win would fain have a fine young father i' law with a feather, that her mother might hood it, and chain it, with Mistress Overdo. But you do not take the right course, Master Winwife.

WINWIFE.

No? Master Littlewit, why?

LITTLEWIT.

You are not mad enough.

WINWIFE.

How? Is madness a right course?

LITTLEWIT.

I say nothing, but I wink upon Win. You have a friend, one Master Quarlous, comes here sometimes?

WINWIFE.

Why? he makes no love to her, does he?

LITTLEWIT.

Not a tokenworth that ever I saw, I assure you, but—

WINWIFE.

What?

LITTLEWIT.

He is the more madcap o' the two. You do not apprehend me.

WIN.

You have a hot coal i' your mouth now, you cannot hold.

LITTLEWIT.

Let me out with it, dear Win.

WIN.

I'll tell him myself.

32. one Master Quarlous] *G.;* one (Master *Quarlous*) *F.*

---

25. *feather . . . hood . . . chain*] marks of civic office (cf. IV.iv.149).

34. *tokenworth*] the smallest amount; a token was a piece of metal given by tradesmen to make up for a scarcity of small coin; since "token" also meant the plague and venereal disease, Littlewit may be quibbling.

LITTLEWIT.

Do, and take all the thanks, and much good do thy pretty heart, Win.

WIN.

Sir, my mother has had her nativity-water cast lately by the cunning men in Cow-lane, and they ha' told her her fortune, and do ensure her she shall never have happy hour, unless she marry within this sen'night, and when it is, it must be a madman, they say.

LITTLEWIT.

Aye, but it must be a gentleman madman.

WIN.

Yes, so the tother man of Moorfields says.

WINWIFE.

But does she believe 'em?

LITTLEWIT.

Yes, and has been at Bedlam twice since, every day, to inquire if any gentleman be there, or to come there, mad!

WINWIFE.

Why, this is a confederacy, a mere piece of practice upon her, by these impostors!

LITTLEWIT.

I tell her so; or else say I that they mean some young madcap-gentleman (for the devil can equivocate, as well as a shopkeeper) and therefore would I advise you to be a little madder than Master Quarlous, hereafter.

WINWIFE.

Where is she? Stirring yet?

LITTLEWIT.

Stirring! Yes, and studying an old elder, come from Banbury, a suitor that puts in here at meal-tide, to praise the

41. good do] *W.*; do good *F.*

---

43. *water cast*] properly urine tested to diagnose a disease; here, a horoscope (nativity).

44. *Cow-lane*] now King Street running from Holborn to Snow Hill.

45. *ensure*] assure.

51. *Bedlam*] St. Mary of Bethlehem's hospital in Bishopsgate, used as a madhouse and visited as one of the entertaining sights of London.

61. *meal-tide*] a jibe at Puritans who substituted "tide" (as in Christ-tide) for "mass" (Christmas); also a quibble on tide = time.

painful brethren, or pray that the sweet singers may be restor'd; says a grace as long as his breath lasts him! Sometime the spirit is so strong with him, it gets quite out of him, and then my mother, or Win, are fain to fetch it again with malmsey, or *aqua coelestis.*

WIN.

Yes indeed, we have such a tedious life with him for his diet, and his clothes too; he breaks his buttons, and cracks seams at every saying he sobs out.

LITTLEWIT.

He cannot abide my vocation, he says.

WIN.

No, he told my mother a Proctor was a claw of the Beast, and that she had little less than committed abomination in marrying me so as she has done.

LITTLEWIT.

Every line, he says, that a Proctor writes, when it comes to be read in the Bishop's court, is a long black hair, kemb'd out of the tail of Antichrist.

WINWIFE.

When came this proselyte?

LITTLEWIT.

Some three days since.

[I.iii] [*Enter to them*] Quarlous.

QUARLOUS.

O sir, ha' you ta'en soil here? It's well a man may reach you after three hours running, yet! What an unmerciful companion art thou, to quit thy lodging at such ungentle-

[I.iii]
3–4. ungentlemanly] ***F***$_3$; vngentle manly ***F***.

---

62. *painful*] diligent.

62. *sweet singers*] Puritans were called so after the Geneva Bible's reference to David (2 Samuel xxiii:1).

66. *malmsey*] a rich, sweet wine.

66. *aqua coelestis*] a cordial distilled from wine.

76. *kemb'd*] combed.

[I.iii]

1. *ta'en soil*] taken refuge (a hunting term).

manly hours! None but a scatter'd covey of fiddlers, or one of these rag-rakers in dunghills, or some marrow-bone man at most, would have been up when thou wert gone abroad, by all description. I pray thee what ailest thou, thou canst not sleep? Hast thou thorns i' thy eye-lids, or thistles i' thy bed?

WINWIFE.

I cannot tell: it seems you had neither i' your feet, that took this pain to find me.

QUARLOUS.

No, and I had, all the lyam-hounds o' the City should have drawn after you by the scent rather. Master John Littlewit! God save you, sir. 'Twas a hot night with some of us, last night, John: shall we pluck a hair o' the same wolf today, Proctor John?

LITTLEWIT.

Do you remember, Master Quarlous, what we discours'd on last night?

QUARLOUS.

Not I, John: nothing that I either discourse or do; at those times I forfeit all to forgetfulness.

LITTLEWIT.

No? not concerning Win? Look you: there she is, and dress'd as I told you she should be; hark you, sir, had you forgot?

QUARLOUS.

By this head, I'll beware how I keep you company, John, when I am drunk, and you have this dangerous memory! That's certain.

WINWIFE.

Why, sir?

QUARLOUS.

Why? We were all a little stain'd last night, sprinkled

25. I am drunk] F_3; I drunke *F.*
27. WINWIFE] IOH. *F; E.A.H. points out that, as* "Proctor John here" *(l. 29) indicates, Winwife, not Littlewit, breaks in here.*

---

5. *rag-rakers*] tramps looking for rags and bones.
12. *lyam-hounds*] bloodhounds.
15–16. *hair . . . wolf*] "Our Ale-Knights often say, Giue us a haire of the dog that last bit us" when asking for a drink of the same liquor (Cotgrave, s.v. *Beste*).
28. *stain'd*] tipsy.

with a cup or two, and I agreed with Proctor John here to come and do somewhat with Win (I know not what 'twas) today; and he puts me in mind on't, now; he says he was coming to fetch me; before truth, if you have that fearful quality, John, to remember, when you are sober, John, what you promise drunk, John, I shall take heed of you, John. For this once, I am content to wink at you; where's your wife? Come hither, Win. *He kisseth her.*

WIN.

Why, John! do you see this, John? Look you! help me, John.

LITTLEWIT.

O Win, fie, what do you mean, Win? Be womanly, Win; make an outcry to your mother, Win? Master Quarlous is an honest gentleman, and our worshipful good friend, Win, and he is Master Winwife's friend too: and Master Winwife comes a suitor to your mother, Win, as I told you before, Win, and may perhaps be our father, Win: they'll do you no harm, Win, they are both our worshipful good friends. Master Quarlous! You must know Master Quarlous, Win; you must not quarrel with Master Quarlous, Win.

QUARLOUS.

No, we'll kiss again and fall in.

LITTLEWIT.

Yes, do, good Win.

WIN.

I' faith you are a fool, John.

LITTLEWIT.

A fool-John she calls me, do you mark that, gentlemen? Pretty littlewit of velvet! A fool-John!

QUARLOUS.

She may call you an apple-John, if you use this.

WINWIFE.

Pray thee forbear, for my respect somewhat.

---

49. *fall in*] become reconciled.

54. *apple-John*] an apple eaten when shriveled after two years keeping; G. suggests a quibble on *apple squire*, pimp.

QUARLOUS.

Hoy-day! How respective you are become o' the sudden! I fear this family will turn you reformed too; pray you come about again. Because she is in possibility to be your daughter-in-law, and may ask you blessing hereafter, when she courts it to Tottenham to eat cream—well, I will forbear, sir; but i' faith, would thou wouldst leave thy exercise of widow-hunting once, this drawing after an old reverend smock by the splay-foot! There cannot be an ancient tripe or trillibub i' the town, but thou art straight nosing it; and 'tis a fine occupation thou'lt confine thyself to, when thou hast got one—scrubbing a piece of buff, as if thou hadst the perpetuity of Pannyer-alley to stink in, or perhaps, worse, currying a carcass that thou hast bound thyself to alive. I'll be sworn, some of them, that thou art or hast been a suitor to, are so old as no chaste or married pleasure can ever become 'em: the honest instrument of procreation has, forty years since, left to belong to 'em; thou must visit 'em, as thou wouldst do a tomb, with a torch, or three handfuls of link, flaming hot, and so thou mayst hap to make 'em feel thee, and after, come to inherit according to thy inches. A sweet course for a man to waste the brand of life for, to be still raking himself a fortune in an old woman's embers; we shall ha' thee, after thou hast been but a month married to one of 'em, look like the quartan ague and the black

---

56. *respective*] careful (of manners).

60. *Tottenham*] probably Tottenham Court, like Hoxton (I.ii.6.n), a favorite place to buy cakes and cream.

62. *drawing after*] tracking by the scent.

64. *tripe or trillibub*] the entrails; also a jeering name for a fat man (Grose).

65. *occupation*] probably a play on *occupy*, have sexual intercourse with (cf. *Ep.*, 117).

67. *buff*] leather; bare skin ("Stripped to the buff").

67. *Pannyer-alley*] an alley out of *Pater Noster Row*; connected with either the selling or making of leather.

68. *currying*] rubbing down (a horse).

74. *link*] torch made of tow and pitch.

80. *quartan ague*] fever in which a paroxysm occurs every fourth day.

jaundice met in a face, and walk as if thou hadst borrow'd legs of a spinner, and voice of a cricket. I would endure to hear fifteen sermons a week 'fore her, and such coarse and loud ones as some of 'em must be; I would e'en desire of Fate, I might dwell in a drum, and take in my sustenance with an old broken tobacco-pipe and a straw. Dost thou ever think to bring thine ears or stomach to the patience of a dry grace, as long as thy tablecloth, and dron'd out by thy son here, that might be thy father, till all the meat o' thy board has forgot it was that day i' the kitchen? Or to brook the noise made, in a question of predestination, by the good laborers and painful eaters assembled together, put to 'em by the matron, your spouse, who moderates with a cup of wine, ever and anon, and a sentence out of Knox between? Or the perpetual spitting, before and after a sober drawn exhortation of six hours, whose better part was the hum-ha-hum? Or to hear prayers groan'd out, over thy iron-chests, as if they were charms to break 'em? And all this, for the hope of two apostle-spoons, to suffer! And a cup to eat a caudle in! For that will be thy legacy. She'll ha' convey'd her state, safe enough from thee, an' she be a right widow.

WINWIFE.

Alas, I am quite off that scent now.

QUARLOUS.

How so?

83. 'fore] *E.A.H.*; for *F.*

---

81. *jaundice*] caused by obstruction of the bile and called black or yellow according to the resulting color of the skin.

82. *spinner*] spider.

83. *'fore*] in preference to.

88. *dry*] plain; thirsty (Puritans favored very long graces before meals).

96. *drawn*] drawn out.

100. *apostle-spoons*] silver, with the figure of an apostle on the handle, a common present of sponsors at baptism; since genuine Puritans would be likely to consider such presents profane, Dame Purecraft's devotion seems spurious.

100. *caudle*] a warm concoction for sick persons.

101–102. *convey'd her state*] made her estate over to another.

WINWIFE.

Put off by a brother of Banbury, one that, they say, is come here and governs all, already.

QUARLOUS.

What do you call him? I knew divers of those Banburians when I was in Oxford.

WINWIFE.

Master Littlewit can tell us.

LITTLEWIT.

Sir! Good Win, go in, and if Master Bartholomew Cokes his man come for the license (the little old fellow), let him speak with me; what say you, gentlemen? [*Exit* Win.]

WINWIFE.

What call you the reverend elder you told me of? your Banbury man.

LITTLEWIT.

Rabbi Busy, sir, he is more than an elder, he is a prophet, sir.

QUARLOUS.

O, I know him! A baker, is he not?

LITTLEWIT.

He was a baker, sir, but he does dream now, and see visions; he has given over his trade.

QUARLOUS.

I remember that too: out of a scruple he took, that (in spic'd conscience) those cakes he made were serv'd to bridals, maypoles, morrises, and such profane feasts and meetings; his Christian name is Zeal-of-the-land.

LITTLEWIT.

Yes, sir, Zeal-of-the-land Busy.

WINWIFE.

How, what a name's there!

LITTLEWIT.

O, they have all such names, sir; he was witness for Win

---

121. *spic'd*] over-scrupulous.

122. *maypoles*] a "stinking Ydol" to a fanatic like Stubbes, *Anatomie of Abuses*, ed. Furnivall, I, 149.

122. *morrises*] morris-dances.

here (they will not be call'd godfathers), and nam'd her Win-the-fight; you thought her name had been Winifred, did you not?

WINWIFE.

I did indeed.

LITTLEWIT.

He would ha' thought himself a stark reprobate, if it had.

QUARLOUS.

Aye, for there was a blue-starch-woman o' the name, at the same time. A notable hypocritical vermin it is; I know him. One that stands upon his face more than his faith, at all times; ever in seditious motion, and reproving for vainglory; of a most lunatic conscience, and spleen, and affects the violence of singularity in all he does (he has undone a grocer here, in Newgate-market, that broke with him, trusted him with currants, as arrant a zeal as he, that's by the way); by his profession, he will ever be i' the state of innocence, though, and childhood; derides all antiquity; defies any other learning than inspiration; and what discretion soever years should afford him, it is all prevented in his original ignorance; ha' not to do with him: for he is a fellow of a most arrogant and invincible dullness, I assure you; who is this?

[I.iv] [*Enter to them*] Wasp, [Win].

WASP.

By your leave, gentlemen, with all my heart to you, and

---

132. *blue-starch-woman*] in a violent passage on the evil of luxurious dress Stubbes calls starch the "deuils liquore" (I, 70); laundresses who would use such liquor on such clothes would be doubly suspect; Nightingale later (II.iv.13) advertises *Goose-green Starch, and the Devil,* a "goodly Ballad against Pride."

134. *stands upon*] depends on.

134. *face*] outward appearance; effrontery.

138. *Newgate-market*] on the south side of Newgate Street.

140. *profession*] declaration of faith.

140–141. *ever . . . innocence*] some Puritans believed that their faith kept them in a state of grace once they were baptized.

141. *childhood*] as a child of God; also extreme Puritans reckoned their age from their "baptism in faith."

144. *prevented*] forestalled.

God you good morrow; Master Littlewit, my business is to you. Is this license ready?

LITTLEWIT.

Here, I ha' it for you, in my hand, Master Humphrey.

WASP.

That's well, nay, never open, or read it to me, it's labor in vain, you know. I am no clerk, I scorn to be sav'd by my book, i' faith I'll hang first; fold it up o' your word and gi' it me; what must you ha' for't?

LITTLEWIT.

We'll talk of that anon, Master Humphrey.

WASP.

Now, or not at all, good Master Proctor, I am for no anons, I assure you.

LITTLEWIT.

Sweet Win, bid Solomon send me the little black box within, in my study.

WASP.

Aye, quickly, good mistress, I pray you; for I have both eggs o' the spit, and iron i' the fire. Say what you must have, good Master Littlewit. [*Exit* Win.]

LITTLEWIT.

Why, you know the price, Master Numps.

WASP.

I know? I know nothing. Aye, what tell you me of knowing, now I am in haste? Sir, I do not know, and I will not know, and I scorn to know, and yet (now I think on't) I will, and do know, as well as another; you must have a mark for your thing here, and eightpence for the box; I could ha' sav'd twopence i' that, an' I had brought it myself, but here's fourteen shillings for you. Good Lord!

23. brought] *H.S.*, XI, 612; bought *F.*

---

2. *God you*] God give you.

6–7. *sav'd by my book*] exempted from the penalty for a crime, as Jonson himself was, after killing Gabriel Spencer (H.S., I, 18) by pleading benefit of clergy—that is, showing one can read.

14–15. *I have . . . spit*] I am very busy.

17. *Numps*] corruption of Humphrey.

22. *mark*] 13*s*. 4*d*.

how long your little wife stays! Pray God, Solomon, your clerk, be not looking i' the wrong box, Master Proctor.

LITTLEWIT.

Good i' faith! no, I warrant you, Solomon is wiser than so, sir.

WASP.

Fie, fie, fie, by your leave, Master Littlewit, this is scurvy, idle, foolish and abominable, with all my heart; I do not like it.

WINWIFE.

Do you hear? Jack Littlewit, what business does thy pretty head think this fellow may have, that he keeps such a coil with?

QUARLOUS.

More than buying of gingerbread i' the Cloister, here (for that we allow him), or a gilt pouch i' the Fair?

LITTLEWIT.

Master Quarlous, do not mistake him: he is his master's both-hands, I assure you.

QUARLOUS.

What? to pull on his boots, a-mornings, or his stockings, does he?

LITTLEWIT.

Sir, if you have a mind to mock him, mock him softly, and look t' other way: for if he apprehend you flout him once, he will fly at you presently. A terrible testy old fellow, and his name is Wasp too.

QUARLOUS.

Pretty insect! make much on him.

WASP.

A plague o' this box, and the pox too, and on him that made it, and her that went for't, and all that should ha' sought it, sent it, or brought it! Do you see, sir?

LITTLEWIT.

Nay, good Master Wasp.

33–34. *keeps . . . a coil*] makes a fuss.
35. *Cloister*] a market for various wares during the Fair.
38. *both-hands*] more than just right-hand man.

WASP.

Good Master Hornet, turd i' your teeth, hold you your tongue; do not I know you? Your father was a 'pothecary, and sold glisters, more than he gave, I wusse: and turd i' your little wife's teeth too; here she comes; 'twill make her spit, as fine as she is, for all her velvet-custard on her head, sir.

[*Re-enter* Win.]

LITTLEWIT.

O! be civil, Master Numps.

WASP.

Why, say I have a humor not to be civil; how then? Who shall compel me? You?

LITTLEWIT.

Here is the box, now.

WASP.

Why a pox o' your box, once again: let your little wife stale in it, and she will. Sir, I would have you to understand, and these gentlemen too, if they please—

WINWIFE.

With all our hearts, sir.

WASP.

That I have a charge. Gentlemen.

LITTLEWIT.

They do apprehend, sir.

WASP.

Pardon me, sir, neither they nor you can apprehend me yet. (You are an ass.) I have a young master, he is now upon his making and marring; the whole care of his well-doing is now mine. His foolish schoolmasters have done nothing but run up and down the country with him, to beg puddings, and cake-bread, of his tenants, and

---

52. *glisters*] clysters.
52. *I wusse*] truly (O. E. *gewis*).
54. *custard*] an open pie of meat or fruit.
57. *humor*] here, inclination; but cf. *E.M.O.*, Induction, ll. 88–117.
61. *stale*] urinate (said of horses).
71. *puddings*] sausages.

almost spoiled him; he has learn'd nothing, but to sing catches, and repeat *Rattle bladder rattle,* and *O, Madge.* I dare not let him walk alone, for fear of learning of vile tunes, which he will sing at supper, and in the sermon-times! If he meet but a carman i' the street, and I find him not talk to keep him off on him, he will whistle him, and all his tunes over, at night in his sleep! He has a head full of bees! I am fain now, for this little time I am absent, to leave him in charge with a gentlewoman; 'tis true, she is a Justice of Peace his wife, and a gentlewoman o' the hood, and his natural sister: but what may happen, under a woman's government, there's the doubt. Gentlemen, you do not know him: he is another manner of piece than you think for! but nineteen year old, and yet he is taller than either of you, by the head, God bless him.

QUARLOUS.

Well, methinks, this is a fine fellow!

WINWIFE.

He has made his master a finer by this description, I should think.

QUARLOUS.

'Faith, much about one; it's cross and pile, whether for a new farthing.

WASP.

I'll tell you, gentlemen—

LITTLEWIT.

Will't please you drink, Master Wasp?

WASP.

Why, I ha' not talk'd so long to be dry, sir, you see no dust or cobwebs come out o' my mouth: do you? You'd ha' me gone, would you?

---

73. *Rattle bladder rattle*] a silly tongue twister.
73. *O, Madge*] a ballad about a barn owl popularly called Madge.
79. *bees*] crazy ideas.
82. *hood*] the mark of her husband's dignity as Justice.
85. *piece*] person.
90. *one*] the same.
90. *cross and pile*] a toss-up; that is, across and with nap or pile of cloth.
90. *whether*] whichever of the two.

LITTLEWIT.

No, but you were in haste e'en now, Master Numps.

WASP.

What an' I were? so I am still, and yet I will stay too; meddle you with your match, your Win, there, she has as little wit as her husband it seems: I have others to talk to.

LITTLEWIT.

She's my match indeed, and as little wit as I, good!

WASP.

We ha' been but a day and a half in town, gentlemen, 'tis true; and yesterday i' the afternoon, we walk'd London, to show the city to the gentlewoman he shall marry, Mistress Grace; but, afore I will endure such another half day, with him, I'll be drawn with a good gib-cat through the great pond at home, as his uncle Hodge was! Why, we could not meet that heathen thing, all day, but stay'd him: he would name you all the signs over, as he went, aloud: and where he spied a parrot, or a monkey, there he was pitch'd, with all the little-long-coats about him, male and female; no getting him away! I thought he would ha' run mad o' the black boy in Bucklersbury, that takes the scurvy, roguy tobacco, there.

LITTLEWIT.

You say true, Master Numps: there's such a one indeed.

WASP.

It's no matter whether there be or no, what's that to you?

QUARLOUS.

He will not allow of John's reading at any hand.

[I.v] [*Enter to them*] Cokes, Mistress Overdo, Grace.

COKES.

O Numps! are you here, Numps? Look where I am,

---

106. *gib-cat*] a practical joke played on a rustic after betting that a cat could pull him through a pond: the pranksters tie one end of a rope around him, the other around a cat, which, guided (and helped) by them, pulls him through the water.

111. *little-long-coats*] children in petticoats.

113. *Bucklersbury*] "possessed of Grocers and Apothecaries" (Stow, I, 260); the latter sold tobacco, then a new fashion.

117. *reading*] comment.

Numps! And Mistress Grace, too! Nay, do not look angerly, Numps: my sister is here, and all, I do not come without her.

WASP.

What the mischief, do you come with her? Or she with you?

COKES.

We came all to seek you, Numps.

WASP.

To seek me? Why, did you all think I was lost? Or run away with your fourteen shillings' worth of small ware here? Or that I had chang'd it i' the Fair, for hobby-horses? 'Sprecious—to seek me!

MRS. OVERDO.

Nay, good Master Numps, do you show discretion, though he be exorbitant, as Master Overdo says, and't be but for conservation of the peace.

WASP.

Marry gip, goody she-Justice, Mistress French-hood! Turd i' your teeth; and turd i' your French-hood's teeth, too, to do you service, do you see? Must you quote your Adam to me! You think you are Madam Regent still, Mistress Overdo, when I am in place? No such matter, I assure you; your reign is out, when I am in, dame.

MRS. OVERDO.

I am content to be in abeyance, sir, and be govern'd by you; so should he too, if he did well; but 'twill be expected you should also govern your passions.

2–3. *angerly*] angrily.

10–11. *hobbyhorses*] toy horses; wenches.

11. *'Sprecious*] by God's precious blood.

13. *exorbitant*] abnormal.

15. *Marry gip*] the oath "By St. Mary of Egypt" confused with *gip*, "gee-up" for a horse.

15. *French-hood*] with "front band depressed over forehead and raised in folds or loops over temples" (*OED*).

18. *Regent*] governor surrogate (in absence of the constituted governor).

21. *abeyance*] in law, the position of waiting for a claimant.

WASP.

Will't so forsooth? Good Lord! how sharp you are! With being at Bet'lem yesterday? Whetstone has set an edge upon you, has he?

MRS. OVERDO.

Nay, if you know not what belongs to your dignity: I do, yet, to mine.

WASP.

Very well, then.

COKES.

Is this the license, Numps? For love's sake, let me see't. I never saw a license.

WASP.

Did you not so? Why, you shall not see't, then.

COKES.

An' you love me, good Numps.

WASP.

Sir, I love you, and yet I do not love you, i' these fooleries; set your heart at rest; there's nothing in't but hard words: and what would you see't for?

COKES.

I would see the length and the breadth on't, that's all; and I will see't now, so I will.

WASP.

You sha' not see it, here.

COKES.

Then I'll see't at home, and I'll look upo' the case here.

WASP.

Why, do so; a man must give way to him a little in trifles, gentlemen. These are errors, diseases of youth: which he will mend, when he comes to judgment, and knowledge of matters. I pray you conceive so, and I thank you. And I pray you pardon him, and I thank you again.

QUARLOUS.

Well, this dry nurse, I say still, is a delicate man.

---

25. *Bet'lem*] cf. I.ii.51.n.

25. *Whetstone*] possibly the name of a keeper at Bedlam; certainly a pun on the whetstone's sharpening ability (G.).

46. *delicate*] courteous.

WINWIFE.

And I am for the cosset, his charge! Did you ever see a fellow's face more accuse him for an ass?

QUARLOUS.

Accuse him? It confesses him one without accusing. What pity 'tis yonder wench should marry such a cokes!

WINWIFE.

'Tis true.

QUARLOUS.

She seems to be discreet, and as sober as she is handsome.

WINWIFE.

Aye, and if you mark her, what a restrain'd scorn she casts upon all his behavior, and speeches!

COKES.

Well, Numps, I am now for another piece of business more, the Fair, Numps, and then—

WASP.

Bless me! deliver me, help, hold me! the Fair!

COKES.

Nay, never fidge up and down, Numps, and vex itself. I am resolute Bartholomew, in this: I'll make no suit on't to you; 'twas all the end of my journey, indeed, to show Mistress Grace my Fair: I call't my Fair, because of Bartholomew: you know my name is Bartholomew, and Bartholomew Fair.

LITTLEWIT.

That was mine afore, gentlemen: this morning. I had that i' faith, upon his license, believe me, there he comes after me.

QUARLOUS.

Come, John, this ambitious wit of yours, I am afraid, will do you no good i' the end.

LITTLEWIT.

No, why, sir?

QUARLOUS.

You grow so insolent with it, and overdoing, John, that

---

47. *cosset*] pet-lamb; spoilt child.
58. *fidge*] pace restlessly.

if you look not to it, and tie it up, it will bring you to some obscure place in time, and there 'twill leave you.

WINWIFE.

Do not trust it too much, John; be more sparing, and use it but now and then; a wit is a dangerous thing, in this age; do not overbuy it.

LITTLEWIT.

Think you so, gentlemen? I'll take heed on't, hereafter.

WIN.

Yes, do, John.

COKES.

A pretty little soul, this same Mistress Littlewit! would I might marry her.

GRACE [*aside*].

So would I, or anybody else, so I might 'scape you.

COKES.

Numps, I will see it, Numps, 'tis decreed: never be melancholy for the matter.

WASP.

Why, see it, sir, see it, do see it! Who hinders you? Why do you not go see it? 'Slid, see it.

COKES.

The Fair, Numps, the Fair.

WASP.

Would the Fair and all the drums and rattles in't were i' your belly for me; they are already i' your brain: he that had the means to travel your head, now, should meet finer sights than any are i' the Fair and make a finer voyage on't, to see it all hung with cockleshells, pebbles, fine wheat-straws, and here and there a chicken's feather, and a cobweb.

QUARLOUS.

Good faith, he looks, methinks, an' you mark him, like one that were made to catch flies, with his Sir Cranion legs.

---

75. *overbuy*] pay too much for.
84. *'slid*] by God's eyelid.
94. *Sir Cranion*] crane-fly; daddy longlegs.

WINWIFE.
And his Numps, to flap 'em away.

WASP.
God be wi' you, sir, there's your bee in a box, and much good do't you.

COKES.
Why, your friend, and Bartholomew; an' you be so contumacious.

QUARLOUS.
What mean you, Numps?

WASP.
I'll not be guilty, I, gentlemen.

MRS. OVERDO.
You will not let him go, brother, and lose him?

COKES.
Who can hold that will away? I had rather lose him than the Fair, I wusse.

WASP.
You do not know the inconvenience, gentlemen, you persuade to: nor what trouble I have with him in these humors. If he go to the Fair, he will buy of everything to a baby there; and household-stuff for that too. If a leg or an arm on him did not grow on, he would lose it i' the press. Pray heaven I bring him off with one stone! And then he is such a ravener after fruit! You will not believe what a coil I had, t'other day, to compound a business between a Catherine-pear-woman and him, about snatching! 'Tis intolerable, gentlemen!

WINWIFE.
O! but you must not leave him, now, to these hazards, Numps.

WASP.
Nay, he knows too well I will not leave him, and that makes him presume: well, sir, will you go now? If you have such an itch i' your feet to foot it to the Fair, why

---

99–100. *contumacious*] insubordinate.
111. *stone*] testicle. 113. *coil*] fuss.
114. *Catherine-pear*] a small, early pear.

do you stop; am I your tarriers? Go, will you go? Sir, why do you not go?

COKES.

O Numps! have I brought you about? Come, Mistress Grace, and sister, I am resolute Bat, i' faith, still.

GRACE.

Truly, I have no such fancy to the Fair; nor ambition to see it; there's none goes thither of any quality or fashion.

COKES.

O Lord, sir! You shall pardon me, Mistress Grace, we are enow of ourselves to make it a fashion: and for qualities, let Numps alone, he'll find qualities.

[*Exeunt* Cokes, Wasp, Grace, Mistress Overdo.]

QUARLOUS.

What a rogue in apprehension is this! to understand her language no better.

WINWIFE.

Aye, and offer to marry to her? Well, I will leave the chase of my widow, for today, and directly to the Fair. These flies cannot, this hot season, but engender us excellent creeping sport.

QUARLOUS.

A man that has but a spoonful of brain would think so. Farewell, John. [*Exeunt* Quarlous, Winwife.]

LITTLEWIT.

Win, you see, 'tis in fashion, to go to the Fair, Win: we must to the Fair too, you and I, Win. I have an affair i' the Fair, Win, a puppet-play of mine own making (say nothing) that I writ for the motion-man, which you must see, Win.

WIN.

I would I might, John, but my mother will never consent to such a "profane motion," she will call it.

LITTLEWIT.

Tut, we'll have a device, a dainty one (now, Wit, help at a pinch, good Wit come, come, good Wit, and't be thy

---

121. *tarriers*] delayers. 126. *quality*] social rank. 128. *enow*] enough.
129. *qualities*] characteristics. 130. *apprehension*] understanding.
135. *creeping*] stealthy? 141. *motion-man*] puppet-master.

will). I have it, Win, I have it i' faith, and 'tis a fine one. Win, long to eat of a pig, sweet Win, i' the Fair, do you see? I' the heart o' the Fair; not at Pie-corner. Your mother will do anything, Win, to satisfy your longing, you know; pray thee long, presently, and be sick o' the sudden, good Win. I'll go in and tell her; cut thy lace i' the meantime, and play the hypocrite, sweet Win.

WIN.

No, I'll not make me unready for it. I can be hypocrite enough, though I were never so strait-lac'd.

LITTLEWIT.

You say true, you have been bred i' the family, and brought up to't. Our mother is a most elect hypocrite, and has maintain'd us all this seven year with it, like gentlefolks.

WIN.

Aye, let her alone, John, she is not a wise willful widow for nothing, nor a sanctified sister for a song. And let me alone too, I ha' somewhat o' the mother in me, you shall see, fetch her, fetch her, ah, ah. [*Exit* Littlewit.]

[I.vi] [*Enter to her*] Purecraft, Littlewit.

PURECRAFT.

Now, the blaze of the beauteous discipline fright away this evil from our house! How now, Win-the-fight, child: how do you? Sweet child, speak to me.

WIN.

Yes, forsooth.

PURECRAFT.

Look up, sweet Win-the-fight, and suffer not the enemy to enter you at this door; remember that your education

---

149. *Pie-corner*] on Giltspur Street where the chief cookshops were, but where they would miss the "heart o' the Fair."

152. *cut thy lace*] possibly a play on "cut-work" (open-work lace); cf. III.ii.10.

154. *make . . . unready*] undress.

162. *mother*] hysteria (one part of a triple pun).

[I.vi]

1. *beauteous discipline*] cant phrase for Puritan faith.

has been with the purest; what polluted one was it, that nam'd first the unclean beast, pig, to you, child?

WIN.

Uh, uh.

LITTLEWIT.

Not I, o' my sincerity, mother: she long'd above three hours, ere she would let me know it; who was it, Win?

WIN.

A profane black thing with a beard, John.

PURECRAFT.

O! resist it, Win-the-fight, it is the Tempter, the wicked Tempter, you may know it by the fleshly motion of pig, be strong against it, and its foul temptations, in these assaults, whereby it broacheth flesh and blood, as it were, on the weaker side, and pray against its carnal provocations, good child, sweet child, pray.

LITTLEWIT.

Good mother, I pray you, that she may eat some pig, and her belly full, too; and do not you cast away your own child, and perhaps one of mine, with your tale of the Tempter: how do you, Win? Are you not sick?

WIN.

Yes, a great deal, John (uh, uh).

PURECRAFT.

What shall we do? Call our zealous brother Busy hither, for his faithful fortification in this charge of the adversary; child, my dear child, you shall eat pig, be comforted, my sweet child. [*Exit* Littlewit.]

WIN.

Aye, but i' the Fair, mother.

PURECRAFT.

I mean i' the Fair, if it can be anyway made, or found lawful; where is our brother Busy? Will he not come? Look up, child.

[*Re-enter* Littlewit.]

---

8. *unclean beast*] jibe at the Puritan's literal interpretation of the Old Testament; cf. Deut. xiv:8.

14. *motion*] urging.

16. *broacheth*] pierces.

LITTLEWIT.

Presently, mother, as soon as he has cleans'd his beard. I found him, fast by the teeth i' the cold turkey-pie, i' the cupboard, with a great white loaf on his left hand, and a glass of malmsey on his right.

PURECRAFT.

Slander not the brethren, wicked one.

LITTLEWIT.

Here he is now, purified, mother.

[*Enter*] Busy.

PURECRAFT.

O brother Busy! your help here to edify, and raise us up in a scruple; my daughter Win-the-fight is visited with a natural disease of women call'd, "A longing to eat pig."

LITTLEWIT.

Aye sir, a Bartholomew pig: and in the Fair.

PURECRAFT.

And I would be satisfied from you, religiously-wise, whether a widow of the sanctified assembly, or a widow's daughter, may commit the act, without offense to the weaker sisters.

BUSY.

Verily, for the disease of longing, it is a disease, a carnal disease, or appetite, incident to women; and as it is carnal, and incident, it is natural, very natural. Now pig, it is a meat, and a meat that is nourishing, and may be long'd for, and so consequently eaten; it may be eaten; very exceeding well eaten: but in the Fair, and as a Bartholomew-pig, it cannot be eaten, for the very calling it a Bartholomew-pig, and to eat it so, is a spice of idolatry, and you make the Fair no better than one of the high places. This, I take it, is the state of the question. A high place.

LITTLEWIT.

Aye, but in state of necessity: place should give place,

---

40. *disease*] uneasiness, discomfort. 53. *spice*] species.

54–55. *high places*] E.A.H. aptly cites Levit. xxvi:30 where the Israelites are described as worshiping idols on high places.

Master Busy. (I have a conceit left, yet.)

PURECRAFT.

Good brother Zeal-of-the-land, think to make it as lawful as you can.

LITTLEWIT.

Yes sir, and as soon as you can: for it must be, sir; you see the danger my little wife is in, sir.

PURECRAFT.

Truly, I do love my child dearly, and I would not have her miscarry, or hazard her first fruits, if it might be otherwise.

BUSY.

Surely, it may be otherwise, but it is subject to construction, subject, and hath a face of offense with the weak, a great face, a foul face, but that face may have a veil put over it, and be shadowed, as it were—it may be eaten, and in the Fair, I take it, in a booth, the tents of the wicked: the place is not much, not very much, we may be religious in midst of the profane, so it be eaten with a reformed mouth, with sobriety, and humbleness; not gorg'd in with gluttony, or greediness; there's the fear: for, should she go there, as taking pride in the place, or delight in the unclean dressing, to feed the vanity of the eye, or the lust of the palate, it were not well, it were not fit, it were abominable, and not good.

LITTLEWIT.

Nay, I knew that afore, and told her on't; but courage, Win, we'll be humble enough; we'll seek out the homeliest booth i' the Fair, that's certain; rather than fail, we'll eat it o' the ground.

PURECRAFT.

Aye, and I'll go with you myself, Win-the-fight, and my brother, Zeal-of-the-land, shall go with us too, for our better consolation.

WIN.

Uh, uh.

LITTLEWIT.

Aye, and Solomon too, Win; the more the merrier, Win;

---

67. *face*] outward appearance.

[*aside to Win*] we'll leave Rabbi Busy in a booth.—Solomon, my cloak.

[*Enter*] Solomon.

SOLOMON.

Here, sir.

BUSY.

In the way of comfort to the weak, I will go, and eat. I will eat exceedingly, and prophesy; there may be a good use made of it, too, now I think on't: by the public eating of swine's flesh, to profess our hate and loathing of Judaism, whereof the brethren stand taxed. I will therefore eat, yea, I will eat exceedingly.

LITTLEWIT.

Good, i' faith, I will eat heartily too, because I will be no Jew; I could never away with that stiff-necked generation. And truly, I hope my little one will be like me, that cries for pig so, i' the mother's belly.

BUSY.

Very likely, exceeding likely, very exceeding likely. [*Exeunt.*]

[II.i] [*Enter*] Justice Overdo.

JUSTICE OVERDO.

Well, in Justice' name, and the King's, and for the Commonwealth! defy all the world, Adam Overdo, for a disguise, and all story; for thou hast fitted thyself, I swear: fain would I meet the Lynceus now, that eagle's eye, that piercing Epidaurian serpent (as my Quintus Horace calls him), that could discover a Justice of Peace (and lately of

---

94–95. *Judaism . . . taxed*] because of their concentration on the Old Testament.

98. *away with*] agree with.

[II.i]

1–2. *Commonwealth*] the general good; the "nation."

3. *fitted*] furnished.

4. *Lynceus*] an Argonaut famous for keen sight.

5. *Epidaurian serpent*] Horace in *Sat.* I.iii.26–27 alludes to worship of Aesculapius at Epidaurus, where serpents, supposed to have keen vision, were believed to be incarnations of the god.

the Quorum) under this covering. They may have seen many a fool in the habit of a Justice; but never till now, a Justice in the habit of a fool. Thus must we do, though, that wake for the public good: and thus hath the wise magistrate done in all ages. There is a doing of right out of wrong, if the way be found. Never shall I enough commend a worthy worshipful man, sometime a capital member of this city, for his high wisdom in this point, who would take you, now the habit of a porter; now of a carman; now of the dog-killer, in this month of August; and in the winter, of a seller of tinder-boxes; and what would he do in all these shapes? Marry, go you into every alehouse, and down into every cellar; measure the length of puddings, take the gauge of black pots and cans, aye, and custards, with a stick; and their circumference, with a thread; weigh the loaves of bread on his middle-finger; then would he send for 'em, home; give the puddings to the poor, the bread to the hungry, the custards to his children; break the pots, and burn the cans, himself; he would not trust his corrupt officers; he would do't himself. Would all men in authority would follow this worthy precedent! For (alas) as we are public persons, what do we know? Nay, what can wc know? Wc hear with other men's ears; we see with other men's eyes; a foolish constable, or a sleepy watchman, is all our information: he slanders a gentleman, by the virtue of his place (as he calls it), and we, by the vice of ours, must believe him: as, a while agone, they made me, yea me, to mistake an honest zealous pursuivant, for a seminary; and a proper

28. precedent] *W.*; president *F.*

---

7. *Quorum*] the learned J.P's whose presence was required to constitute a bench.

13. *a worthy . . . man*] possibly, as C.S.A. claims, Sir Thomas Hayes; cf. Induction, l. 145 and note.

16. *dog-killer*] stray dogs were killed as possible carriers of the plague, especially in summer.

35. *pursuivant*] state official empowered to execute warrants for arrest and search.

35. *seminary*] recusant trained in one of the seminaries on the Continent.

young Bachelor of Music, for a bawd. This we are subject to, that live in high place: all our intelligence is idle, and most of our intelligencers knaves; and, by your leave, ourselves thought little better, if not arrant fools, for believing 'em. I, Adam Overdo, am resolv'd therefore to spare spy-money hereafter, and make mine own discoveries. Many are the yearly enormities of this Fair, in whose courts of Pie-powders I have had the honor during the three days sometimes to sit as judge. But this is the special day for detection of those foresaid enormities. Here is my black book for the purpose, this the cloud that hides me: under this covert I shall see, and not be seen. On, Junius Brutus. And as I began, so I'll end: in Justice' name, and the King's; and for the Commonwealth!

[II.ii] [*Enter*] Leatherhead, Trash, *Passengers*.

LEATHERHEAD.

The Fair's pestilence dead, methinks; people come not abroad, today, what ever the matter is. Do you hear, Sister Trash, Lady o' the Basket? Sit farther with your gingerbread-progeny there, and hinder not the prospect of my shop, or I'll ha' it proclaim'd i' the Fair, what stuff they are made on.

TRASH.

Why, what stuff are they made on, Brother Leatherhead? Nothing but what's wholesome, I assure you.

LEATHERHEAD.

Yes, stale bread, rotten eggs, musty ginger, and dead honey, you know.

---

37. *intelligence*] information. 37. *idle*] without foundation.

42. *enormities*] evils.

43. *Pie-powders*] a summary court held at fairs to administer justice among traveling dealers and others temporarily present.

48. *Junius Brutus*] to escape death at the hands of Tarquinius Superbus, he disguised himself as an idiot; later he became so inflexible as a judge that he sentenced his own sons to death for treason (Livy II. v).

[II.ii]

1. *pestilence*] "plaguily." 9. *dead*] flavorless.

JUSTICE OVERDO [*aside*].

Aye! have I met with enormity so soon?

LEATHERHEAD.

I shall mar your market, old Joan.

TRASH.

Mar my market, thou too-proud pedlar? Do thy worst; I defy thee, aye, and thy stable of hobbyhorses. I pay for my ground, as well as thou dost; and thou wrong'st me, for all thou art parcel-poet, and an inginer, I'll find a friend shall right me, and make a ballad of thee, and thy cattel all over. Are you puff'd up with the pride of your wares? Your arsedine?

LEATHERHEAD.

Go to, old Joan, I'll talk with you anon; and take you down too afore Justice Overdo, he is the man must charm you; I'll ha' you i' the Pie-powders.

TRASH.

Charm me? I'll meet thee face to face, afore his worship, when thou dar'st: and though I be a little crooked o' my body, I'll be found as upright in my dealing as any woman in Smithfield; aye, charm me!

JUSTICE OVERDO [*aside*].

I am glad to hear my name is their terror, yet; this is doing of Justice.

LEATHERHEAD.

What do you lack? What is't you buy? What do you lack? Rattles, drums, halberts, horses, babies o' the best? Fiddles o' th' finest?

Enter Costermonger, Nightingale.

31.1. *Enter* Costermonger, Nightingale] G.; *Enter Cost. F.*

---

16. *parcel-poet*] part poet.

16. *inginer*] designer, inventor.

17. *make . . . thee*] a frequent threat (cf. *I Henry IV*, II.ii.43).

18. *cattel*] property.

19. *arsedine*] "gold coloured alloy of copper and zinc, rolled into very thin leaf, and used to ornament toys" (*OED*).

20–21. *take . . . down*] humiliate.

21. *charm*] subdue (silence, as if by magic).

30. *halberts*] battle axes with long handles and spikes projecting above the blades.

COSTERMONGER.

Buy any pears, pears, fine, very fine pears!

TRASH.

Buy any gingerbread, gilt gingerbread!

NIGHTINGALE.

Hey, now the Fair's a filling!
O, for a tune to startle
The birds o' the booths here billing
Yearly with old Saint Bartle!
The drunkards they are wading,
The punks and chapmen trading;
Who'd see the Fair without his lading?

Buy any ballads; new ballads?

[*Enter*] Ursula.

URSULA.

Fie upon't: who would wear out their youth and prime thus, in roasting of pigs, that had any cooler vocation? Hell's a kind of cold cellar to't, a very fine vault, o' my conscience! What, Mooncalf!

MOONCALF [*within*].

Here, Mistress.

NIGHTINGALE.

How now, Urs'la? In a heat, in a heat?

URSULA.

My chair, you false faucet you; and my morning's draught, quickly, a bottle of ale to quench me, rascal. I am all fire, and fat, Nightingale; I shall e'en melt away to the first woman, a rib, again, I am afraid. I do water the ground in knots as I go, like a great garden-pot; you may follow me by the S's I make.

NIGHTINGALE.

Alas, good Urs; was 'Zekiel here this morning?

45. What, Mooncalf!] *G.*; what *Moone-calfe. F.*

---

33. *gilt*] gold leaf was used to decorate gingerbread.
40. *lading*] freight.
48. *faucet*] tap for drawing liquor from a barrel.
52. *knots*] figures formed by criss-crossing lines.

URSULA.

'Zekiel? what 'Zekiel?

NIGHTINGALE.

'Zekiel Edgworth, the civil cutpurse, you know him well enough; he that talks bawdy to you still: I call him my secretary.

URSULA.

He promis'd to be here this morning, I remember.

NIGHTINGALE.

When he comes, bid him stay: I'll be back again presently.

URSULA.

Best take your morning's dew in your belly, Nightingale.

Mooncalf *brings in the chair.*

Come, sir, set it here; did not I bid you should get this chair let out o' the sides, for me, that my hips might play? You'll never think of anything, till your dame be rump-gall'd; 'tis well, changeling: because it can take in your grasshopper's thighs, you care for no more. Now, you look as you had been i' the corner o' the booth, fleaing your breech with a candle's end, and set fire o' the Fair. Fill, stoat: fill.

JUSTICE OVERDO [*aside*].

This pig-woman do I know, and I will put her in, for my second enormity; she hath been before me, punk, pinnace and bawd, any time these two and twenty years, upon record i' the Pie-powders.

URSULA.

Fill again, you unlucky vermin.

MOONCALF.

'Pray you be not angry, mistress, I'll ha' it widen'd anon.

URSULA.

No, no, I shall e'en dwindle away to't, ere the Fair be done, you think, now you ha' heated me? A poor vex'd

58. *secretary*] one entrusted with another's secrets.
66. *gall'd*] chafed.
66. *changeling*] ugly child left by fairies in exchange for a better.
68. *fleaing*] quibble on flaying?
70. *stoat*] weasel; stupid person.
73. *pinnace*] either a whore or a go-between.

thing I am, I feel myself dropping already, as fast as I can: two stone o' suet a day is my proportion: I can but hold life and soul together, with this (here's to you, Nightingale) and a whiff of tobacco, at most. Where's my pipe now? Not fill'd? Thou arrant incubee.

NIGHTINGALE.

Nay, Urs'la, thou'lt gall between the tongue and the teeth, with fretting, now.

URSULA.

How can I hope that ever he'll discharge his place of trust—tapster, a man of reckoning under me—that remembers nothing I say to him? [*Exit* Nightingale.]

But look to't, sirrah, you were best; threepence a pipeful, I will ha' made of all my whole half-pound of tobacco, and a quarter of a pound of coltsfoot mix'd with it too, to eke it out. I that have dealt so long in the fire, will not be to seek in smoke, now. Then, six and twenty shillings a barrel I will advance o' my beer, and fifty shillings a hundred o' my bottle-ale; I ha' told you the ways how to raise it. Froth your cans well i' the filling, at length, rogue, and jog your bottles o' the buttock, sirrah, then skink out the first glass, ever, and drink with all companies, though you be sure to be drunk; you'll mis-reckon the better, and be less asham'd on't. But your true trick, rascal, must be, to be ever busy, and mis-take away the bottles and cans, in haste, before they be half drunk off, and never hear anybody call (if they should chance to mark you), till you ha' brought fresh, and be able to forswear 'em. Give me a drink of ale.

JUSTICE OVERDO [*aside*].

This is the very womb and bed of enormity! gross, as her-

92. eke] *G.*; itch *F*; eech F_3.

---

83. *incubee*] incubus; here perhaps the offspring of intercourse with such a demon.

87. *reckoning*] distinction; adding up charges.

91. *coltsfoot*] long used to adulterate tobacco.

93. *to seek*] wanting.

94. *advance*] raise.

97. *skink*] draw liquor.

self! This must all down for enormity, all, every whit on't. *One knocks.*

URSULA.

Look who's there, sirrah! Five shillings a pig is my price, at least; if it be a sow-pig, sixpence more: if she be a great-bellied wife, and long for't, sixpence more for that.

JUSTICE OVERDO [*aside*].

O tempora! O mores! I would not ha' lost my discovery of this one grievance, for my place, and worship o' the bench. How is the poor subject abus'd, here! Well, I will fall in with her, and with her Mooncalf, and win out wonders of enormity. [*to Ursula*] By thy leave, goodly woman, and the fatness of the Fair: oily as the King's constable's lamp, and shining as his shoeing-horn! Hath thy ale virtue, or thy beer strength? that the tongue of man may be tickled? and his palate pleas'd in the morning? Let thy pretty nephew here go search and see.

URSULA.

What new roarer is this?

MOONCALF.

O Lord! do you not know him, mistress, 'tis mad Arthur of Bradley, that makes the orations. Brave master, old Arthur of Bradley, how do you? Welcome to the Fair; when shall we hear you again, to handle your matters? With your back again' a booth, ha? I ha' been one o' your little disciples, i' my days!

JUSTICE OVERDO.

Let me drink, boy, with my love, thy Aunt, here; that I may be eloquent: but of thy best, lest it be bitter in my mouth, and my words fall foul on the Fair.

URSULA.

Why dost thou not fetch him drink? And offer him to sit?

MOONCALF.

Is't ale, or beer, Master Arthur?

---

112. *O . . . mores*] Cicero *In Catilinam* I.i.2; cf. *C.*, IV.190: "O age, and manners."

113. *worship*] honor.

123. *Arthur*] the hero of "The Ballad on the Wedding of Arthur of Bradley."

129. *Aunt*] gossip; perhaps bawd.

JUSTICE OVERDO.

Thy best, pretty stripling, thy best; the same thy dove drinketh, and thou drawest on holy days.

URSULA.

Bring him a sixpenny bottle of ale; they say, a fool's handsel is lucky.

JUSTICE OVERDO.

Bring both, child. Ale for Arthur, and beer for Bradley. Ale for thine Aunt, boy. [*Exit* Mooncalf.]
[*aside*] My disguise takes to the very wish and reach of it. I shall, by the benefit of this, discover enough, and more —and yet get off with the reputation of what I would be: a certain middling thing, between a fool and a madman.

[II.iii] [*Enter*] Knockem *to them.*

KNOCKEM.

What! my little lean Urs'la! my she-bear! art thou alive yet? With thy litter of pigs, to grunt out another Bartholomew Fair? Ha!

URSULA.

Yes, and to amble afoot, when the Fair is done, to hear you groan out of a cart, up the heavy hill.

KNOCKEM.

Of Holborn, Urs'la, meanst thou so? For what? For what, pretty Urs?

URSULA.

For cutting halfpenny purses, or stealing little penny dogs, out o' the Fair.

KNOCKEM.

O! good words, good words, Urs.

JUSTICE OVERDO [*aside*].

Another special enormity. A cutpurse of the sword! the

---

134. *dove*] darling.

137. *handsel*] the first money taken or first gift received: supposed to bring luck.

[II.iii]

5. *heavy hill*] Holborn Hill, part of the route from the prison at Newgate to the gallows at Tyburn.

boot, and the feather! Those are his marks.

[*Re-enter* Mooncalf.]

URSULA.

You are one of those horse-leeches that gave out I was dead, in Turnbull-street, of a surfeit of bottle-ale, and tripes?

KNOCKEM.

No, 'twas better meat, Urs: cow's udders, cow's udders!

URSULA.

Well, I shall be meet with your mumbling mouth one day.

KNOCKEM.

What? Thou'lt poison me with a newt in a bottle of ale, wilt thou? Or a spider in a tobacco-pipe, Urs? Come, there's no malice in these fat folks, I never fear thee, and I can 'scape thy lean Mooncalf here. Let's drink it out, good Urs, and no vapors! [*Exit* Ursula.]

JUSTICE OVERDO.

Dost thou hear, boy? (There's for thy ale, and the remnant for thee.) Speak in thy faith of a faucet, now; is this goodly person before us here, this vapors, a knight of the knife?

MOONCALF.

What mean you by that, Master Arthur?

JUSTICE OVERDO.

I mean a child of the horn-thumb, a babe of booty, boy; a cutpurse.

MOONCALF.

O Lord, sir! far from it. This is Master Dan Knockem: Jordan the ranger of Turnbull. He is a horse-courser, sir.

JUSTICE OVERDO.

Thy dainty dame, though, call'd him cutpurse.

---

13. *horse-leeches*] farriers; bloodsuckers. 17. *meet*] even.

23. *vapors*] a vague term meaning fantastic notions or foolish bragging or quarreling (Nares).

29. *horn-thumb*] the cutpurse's case worn to protect his thumb from the knife.

32. *Jordan*] chamber pot.

MOONCALF.

Like enough, sir, she'll do forty such things in an hour (an' you listen to her) for her recreation, if the toy take her i' the greasy kerchief: it makes her fat, you see. She battens with it.

JUSTICE OVERDO [*aside*].

Here might I ha' been deceiv'd, now, and ha' put a fool's blot upon myself, if I had not play'd an after-game o' discretion.

Ursula *comes in again dropping.*

KNOCKEM.

Alas, poor Urs, this's an ill season for thee.

URSULA.

Hang yourself, hackney-man.

KNOCKEM.

How? How? Urs, vapors! Motion breed vapors?

URSULA.

Vapors? Never tusk nor twirl your dibble, good Jordan, I know what you'll take to a very drop. Though you be captain o' the roarers, and fight well at the case of piss-pots, you shall not fright me with your lion-chap, sir, nor your tusks; you angry? You are hungry: come, a pig's head will stop your mouth, and stay your stomach, at all times.

KNOCKEM.

Thou art such another mad merry Urs still! Troth I do make conscience of vexing thee now i' the dog-days, this hot weather, for fear of found'ring thee i' the body; and melting down a pillar of the Fair. Pray thee take thy

---

35. *toy*] whim.

39. *after-game*] a second game played to afford a chance of reversing the issue of the first.

43. *Motion*] exertion (elliptical for "does motion breed?").

44. *tusk*] to show the teeth? (*OED*).

44. *dibble*] trowel; here a spade beard (often affected by swash-bucklers).

47. *lion-chap*] lion jaw.

53. *found'ring . . . body*] an eruptive disease got by meat, drink, or labor (*Markhams Maister-peece*, pp. 122–123).

chair again, and keep state; and let's have a fresh bottle of ale, and a pipe of tobacco; and no vapors. I'll ha' this belly o' thine taken up, and thy grass scour'd, wench; look! here's Ezekiel Edgworth; a fine boy of his inches as any is i' the Fair! has still money in his purse, and will pay all, with a kind heart; and good vapors.

[II.iv]

[*Enter*] *to them* Edgworth, Nightingale, Corncutter, Tinderbox-man, *Passengers.*

EDGWORTH.

That I will, indeed, willingly, Master Knockem; fetch some ale, and tobacco. [*Exit* Mooncalf.]

LEATHERHEAD.

What do you lack, gentlemen? Maid: see a fine hobby-horse for your young master: cost you but a token a week his provender.

CORNCUTTER.

Ha' you any corns i' your feet and toes?

TINDERBOX-MAN.

Buy a mousetrap, a mousetrap, or a tormentor for a flea.

TRASH.

Buy some gingerbread.

NIGHTINGALE.

Ballads, ballads! fine new ballads:
Hear for your love, and buy for your money!
A delicate ballad o' *The Ferret and the Coney!*
A Preservative again' the Punks' Evil!
Another of *Goose-green Starch, and the Devil!*
A Dozen of Divine Points, and *The Godly Garters!*

---

55. *keep state*] keep the ceremony due to your dignified position.
57. *taken up*] reduced (a term used in dieting of horses).
57. *scour'd*] purged.

[II.iv]

0.1–2] The Tinderbox-man takes the place of the Mousetrap-man listed in the Persons of the Play.
7. *tormentor*] trap.
13. *Goose-green*] yellowish green.

The Fairing of Good Counsel, of an ell and three quarters!
What is't you buy?
The Windmill blown down by the witch's fart!
Or *Saint George, that O! did break the dragon's heart!*

[*Re-enter* Mooncalf.]

EDGWORTH.

Master Nightingale, come hither, leave your mart a little.

NIGHTINGALE.

O my secretary! What says my secretary?

JUSTICE OVERDO.

Child o' the bottles, what's he? What's he?

MOONCALF.

A civil young gentleman, Master Arthur, that keeps company with the roarers, and disburses all, still. He has ever money in his purse; he pays for them, and they roar for him: one does good offices for another. They call him the secretary, but he serves nobody. A great friend of the ballad-man's, they are never asunder.

JUSTICE OVERDO.

What pity 'tis so civil a young man should haunt this debauch'd company! Here's the bane of the youth of our time apparent. A proper penman, I see't in his countenance; he has a good clerk's look with him, and I warrant him a quick hand.

MOONCALF.

A very quick hand, sir. [*Exit.*]

EDGWORTH.

All the purses and purchase I give you today by conveyance, bring hither to Urs'la's presently. Here we will meet at night in her lodge, and share. Look you choose good places for your standing i' the Fair, when you sing, Nightingale.

21. What's] F_3; what *F*.

---

15. *ell*] forty-five inches; apparently referring to the length of the broadside.

34. *purchase*] booty.

34–35. *conveyance*] transference; contrivance.

This they whisper, that Overdo *hears it not.*

URSULA.

Aye, near the fullest passages; and shift 'em often.

EDGWORTH.

And i' your singing, you must use your hawk's eye nimbly, and fly the purse to a mark still, where 'tis worn and o' which side, that you may gi' me the sign with your beak, or hang your head that way i' the tune.

URSULA.

Enough, talk no more on't: your friendship, masters, is not now to begin. Drink your draught of indenture, your sup of covenant, and away: the Fair fills apace, company begins to come in, and I ha' ne'er a pig ready, yet.

KNOCKEM.

Well said! Fill the cups, and light the tobacco: let's give fire i' th' works, and noble vapors.

EDGWORTH.

And shall we ha' smocks, Urs'la, and good whimsies, ha?

URSULA.

Come, you are i' your bawdy vein! The best the Fair will afford, 'Zekiel, if bawdy Whit keep his word.

[*Re-enter* Mooncalf.]

How do the pigs, Mooncalf?

MOONCALF.

Very passionate, mistress, one on 'em has wept out an eye. Master Arthur o' Bradley is melancholy, here, nobody talks to him. Will you any tobacco, Master Arthur?

JUSTICE OVERDO.

No, boy, let my meditations alone.

MOONCALF.

He's studying for an oration, now.

---

41. *fly . . . to a mark*] said when a falcon marks the spot where its prey disappears from view; cf. III.v.250.

45. *draught of indenture*] since drinking went with the drawing up of agreements, the pun on "draught" was customary.

50. *smocks . . . whimsies*] wenches.

54. *passionate*] sorrowful.

54–55. *wept out an eye*] a sign that a roasting pig is nearly done.

JUSTICE OVERDO [*aside*].

If I can, with this day's travel, and all my policy, but rescue this youth, here, out of the hands of the lewd man, and the strange woman, I will sit down at night, and say with my friend Ovid, *Jamque opus exegi, quod nec Jovis ira, nec ignis, &c.*

KNOCKEM.

Here, 'Zekiel; here's a health to Urs'la, and a kind vapor: thou hast money i' thy purse still; and store! How dost thou come by it? Pray thee vapor thy friends some in a courteous vapor.

EDGWORTH.

Half I have, Master Dan Knockem, is always at your service.

JUSTICE OVERDO [*aside*].

Ha, sweet nature! What goshawk would prey upon such a lamb?

KNOCKEM.

Let's see what 'tis, 'Zekiel! Count it, come, fill him to pledge me.

[II.v] [*Enter*] Winwife, Quarlous, *to them.*

WINWIFE.

We are here before 'em, methinks.

QUARLOUS.

All the better, we shall see 'em come in now.

LEATHERHEAD.

What do you lack, gentlemen, what is't you lack? A fine horse? A lion? A bull? A bear? A dog, or a cat? An excellent fine Bartholomew-bird? Or an instrument? What is't you lack?

---

59. *travel*] travail. 59. *policy*] shrewdness.
61. *strange woman*] harlot.
62–63. *Jamque . . . ignis*] "And now my work is done, which neither the wrath of Jove, nor fire, nor sword, nor the gnawing tooth of time shall ever be able to undo" (Ovid *Met.* XV. 871–872, trans. F. J. Miller).
65. *store*] plenty.

QUARLOUS.

'Slid! here's Orpheus among the beasts, with his fiddle, and all!

TRASH.

Will you buy any comfortable bread, gentlemen?

QUARLOUS.

And Ceres selling her daughter's picture, in gingerwork!

WINWIFE.

That these people should be so ignorant to think us chapmen for 'em! Do we look as if we would buy gingerbread? Or hobbyhorses?

QUARLOUS.

Why, they know no better ware than they have, nor better customers than come. And our very being here makes us fit to be demanded, as well as others. Would Cokes would come! There were a true customer for 'em.

KNOCKEM.

How much is't? Thirty shillings? Who's yonder! Ned Winwife? And Tom Quarlous, I think! Yes. (Gi' me it all, gi' me it all.) Master Winwife! Master Quarlous! Will you take a pipe of tobacco with us? (Do not discredit me now, 'Zekiel.)

WINWIFE.

Do not see him! He is the roaring horse-courser, pray thee let's avoid him: turn down this way.

QUARLOUS.

'Slud, I'll see him, and roar with him too, and he roar'd as loud as Neptune; pray thee go with me.

WINWIFE.

You may draw me to as likely an inconvenience, when you please, as this.

QUARLOUS.

Go to then, come along, we ha' nothing to do, man, but to see sights now.

---

9. *comfortable bread*] sustaining? spiced gingerbread?
12. *chapmen*] customers.
23. *roaring*] brawling.
25. *'Slud*] by God's blood.

KNOCKEM.

Welcome Master Quarlous, and Master Winwife! Will you take any froth, and smoke with us?

QUARLOUS.

Yes, sir, but you'll pardon us if we knew not of so much familiarity between us afore.

KNOCKEM.

As what, sir?

QUARLOUS.

To be so lightly invited to smoke, and froth.

KNOCKEM.

A good vapor! Will you sit down, sir? This is old Urs'la's mansion, how like you her bower? Here you may ha' your punk and your pig in state, sir, both piping hot.

QUARLOUS.

I had rather ha' my punk cold, sir.

JUSTICE OVERDO [*aside*].

There's for me; punk! and pig!

URSULA.

What, Mooncalf? You rogue. *She calls within.*

MOONCALF.

By and by, the bottle is almost off, mistress; here, Master Arthur.

URSULA.

I'll part you and your play-fellow there i' the guarded coat, an' you sunder not the sooner. [*Exit.*]

KNOCKEM.

Master Winwife, you are proud, methinks; you do not talk, nor drink; are you proud?

WINWIFE.

Not of the company I am in, sir, nor the place, I assure you.

KNOCKEM.

You do not except at the company! Do you? Are you in vapors, sir?

---

38. *bower*] decked with boughs; cf. III.ii.55.
40. *punk cold*] that is, not diseased.
45. *guarded*] having "guards" or trimmings of braid.
51–52. *in vapors*] cf. Jonson's description of vapors, IV.iv.27.1–3.

MOONCALF.

Nay, good Master Dan Knockem, respect my mistress' bower, as you call it; for the honor of our booth, none o' your vapors here.

She comes out with a fire-brand.

URSULA.

Why, you thin lean polecat you, and they have a mind to be i' their vapors, must you hinder 'em? What did you know, vermin, if they would ha' lost a cloak, or such a trifle? Must you be drawing the air of pacification here, while I am tormented, within, i' the fire, you weasel?

MOONCALF.

Good mistress, 'twas in the behalf of your booth's credit that I spoke.

URSULA.

Why? Would my booth ha' broke, if they had fall'n out in't, sir? Or would their heat ha' fir'd it? In, you rogue, and wipe the pigs, and mend the fire, that they fall not, or I'll both baste and roast you, till your eyes drop out, like 'em. (Leave the bottle behind you, and be curst a while.) [*Exit* Mooncalf.]

QUARLOUS.

Body o' the Fair! what's this? Mother o' the bawds?

KNOCKEM.

No, she's mother o' the pigs, sir, mother o' the pigs!

WINWIFE.

Mother o' the Furies, I think, by her firebrand.

QUARLOUS.

Nay, she is too fat to be a Fury, sure some walking sow of tallow!

WINWIFE.

An inspir'd vessel of kitchen-stuff! *She drinks this while.*

QUARLOUS.

She'll make excellent gear for the coach-makers, here in Smithfield, to anoint wheels and axle-trees with.

---

63. *broke*] gone bankrupt.
74. *inspir'd*] inflated; infused with divine power.
74. *vessel*] a Puritan phrase for a person filled with some quality.

URSULA.

Aye, aye, gamesters, mock a plain plump soft wench o' the suburbs, do, because she's juicy and wholesome: you must ha' your thin pinch'd ware, pent up i' the compass of a dog-collar (or 'twill not do), that looks like a long lac'd conger, set upright, and a green feather, like fennel, i' the jowl on't.

KNOCKEM.

Well said, Urs, my good Urs; to 'em, Urs.

QUARLOUS.

Is she your quagmire, Dan Knockem? Is this your bog?

NIGHTINGALE.

We shall have a quarrel presently.

KNOCKEM.

How? Bog? Quagmire? Foul vapors! Humh!

QUARLOUS.

Yes, he that would venture for't, I assure him, might sink into her, and be drown'd a week, ere any friend he had could find where he were.

WINWIFE.

And then he would be a fortnight weighing up again.

QUARLOUS.

'Twere like falling into a whole shire of butter: they had need be a team of Dutchmen, should draw him out.

KNOCKEM.

Answer 'em, Urs; where's thy Bartholomew-wit, now? Urs, thy Bartholomew-wit?

URSULA.

Hang 'em, rotten, roguy cheaters, I hope to see 'em plagu'd one day (pox'd they are already, I am sure) with

---

78. *suburbs*] often associated with licentiousness.
81. *lac'd*] streaked.
81. *conger*] sea-eel.
82. *jowl*] fish head.
84. *quagmire . . . bog*] cf. Cunningham's note (Appendix, p. 550): "Every dealer in unsound horses has a prepared corner of his yard in which the 'screws' may stand up to their knees in wet clay."
90. *weighing up*] raising up (of a sunken ship).
92. *Dutchman*] famous for their eating of butter.

lean playhouse poultry, that has the bony rump sticking out like the ace of spades or the point of a partizan, that every rib of 'em is like the tooth of a saw; and will so grate 'em with their hips and shoulders, as (take 'em altogether) they were as good lie with a hurdle.

QUARLOUS.

Out upon her, how she drips! She's able to give a man the sweating sickness with looking on her.

URSULA.

Marry look off, with a patch o' your face; and a dozen i' your breech, though they be o' scarlet, sir. I ha' seen as fine outsides, as either o' yours, bring lousy linings to the brokers, ere now, twice a week!

QUARLOUS.

Do you think there may be a fine new cucking-stool i' the Fair, to be purchas'd? One large enough, I mean. I know there is a pond of capacity for her.

URSULA.

For your mother, you rascal; out, you rogue, you hedge-bird, you pimp, you pannier-man's bastard, you!

QUARLOUS.

Ha, ha, ha.

URSULA.

Do you sneer, you dog's-head, you trendle-tail! You look as you were begotten atop of a cart in harvest-time, when the whelp was hot and eager. Go, snuff after your brother's bitch, Mistress Commodity, that's the livery you wear, 'twill be out at the elbows shortly. It's time you went to't, for the tother remnant.

---

97. *poultry*] whores (Grose).
98. *partizan*] a long-handled, double-bladed spear.
103. *sweating sickness*] violent sweating was long considered the chief specific for venereal disease (Nares).
104–105. *patch . . . breech*] symptoms of venereal disease.
107. *brokers*] dealers in second-hand clothes.
108. *cucking-stool*] for ducking scolds.
110. *pond*] Smithfield pond (cf. Stow, I, 16).
111–112. *hedge-bird*] footpad. 112. *pannier-man*] hawker.
114. *trendle-tail*] dog with a curled tail (hence, no thoroughbred).
117. *Commodity*] something bought; whore (Grose).

KNOCKEM.

Peace, Urs, peace, Urs; they'll kill the poor whale, and make oil of her. Pray thee go in.

URSULA.

I'll see 'em pox'd first, and pil'd, and double pil'd.

WINWIFE.

Let's away; her language grows greasier than her pigs.

URSULA.

Does't so, snotty nose? Good Lord! are you sniveling? You were engender'd on a she-beggar, in a barn, when the bald thrasher, your sire, was scarce warm.

WINWIFE.

Pray thee, let's go.

QUARLOUS.

No, faith; I'll stay the end of her, now: I know she cannot last long; I find by her similes she wanes apace.

URSULA.

Does she so? I'll set you gone. Gi' me my pig-pan hither a little. I'll scald you hence, and you will not go. [*Exit.*]

KNOCKEM.

Gentlemen, these are very strange vapors! And very idle vapors! I assure you.

QUARLOUS.

You are a very serious ass, we assure you.

KNOCKEM.

Humh! Ass? And serious? Nay, then pardon me my vapor. I have a foolish vapor, gentlemen: any man that does vapor me the ass, Master Quarlous—

QUARLOUS.

What then, Master Jordan?

KNOCKEM.

I do vapor him the lie.

QUARLOUS.

Faith, and to any man that vapors me the lie, I do vapor that. [*Strikes him.*]

KNOCKEM.

Nay, then, vapors upon vapors.

---

122. *pil'd*] deprived of hair; bald from venereal disease; with a pile or nap like velvet.

EDGWORTH. NIGHTINGALE.

'Ware the pan, the pan, the pan, she comes with the pan, gentlemen. God bless the woman.

Ursula *comes in, with the scalding-pan. They fight. She falls with it.*

URSULA.

Oh! [*Exeunt* Quarlous, Winwife.]

TRASH.

What's the matter?

JUSTICE OVERDO.

Goodly woman!

MOONCALF.

Mistress!

URSULA.

Curse of hell, that ever I saw these fiends, O! I ha' scalded my leg, my leg, my leg, my leg. I ha' lost a limb in the service! Run for some cream and salad oil, quickly! Are you under-peering, you baboon? Rip off my hose, an' you be men, men, men!

MOONCALF.

Run you for some cream, good mother Joan. I'll look to your basket. [*Exit* Trash.]

LEATHERHEAD.

Best sit up i' your chair, Urs'la. Help, gentlemen.

KNOCKEM.

Be of good cheer, Urs; thou hast hinder'd me the currying of a couple of stallions here, that abus'd the good race-bawd o' Smithfield; 'twas time for 'em to go.

NIGHTINGALE.

I' faith, when the pan came, they had made you run else. (This had been a fine time for purchase, if you had ventur'd.)

EDGWORTH.

Not a whit, these fellows were too fine to carry money.

KNOCKEM.

Nightingale, get some help to carry her leg out o' the air;

157–158. *Currying*] dressing down; beating.
161. *purchase*] robbery.

take off her shoes; body o' me, she has the mallanders, the scratches, the crown scab, and the quitter bone, i' the tother leg.

URSULA.

O! the pox, why do you put me in mind o' my leg, thus to make it prick and shoot? Would you ha' me i' the Hospital, afore my time?

KNOCKEM.

Patience, Urs. Take a good heart, 'tis but a blister, as big as a windgall; I'll take it away with the white of an egg, a little honey, and hog's grease; ha' thy pasterns well roll'd and thou shalt pace again by tomorrow. I'll tend thy booth and look to thy affairs, the while: thou shalt sit i' thy chair, and give directions, and shine Ursa major.

[*Exeunt* Knockem, Mooncalf, Ursula.]

[II.vi] [*Enter*] Cokes, Wasp, Mistress Overdo, Grace.

JUSTICE OVERDO.

These are the fruits of bottle-ale, and tobacco! the foam of the one, and the fumes of the other! Stay, young man, and despise not the wisdom of these few hairs, that are grown gray in care of thee.

EDGWORTH.

Nightingale, stay a little. Indeed I'll hear some o' this!

COKES.

Come, Numps, come, where are you? Welcome into the Fair, Mistress Grace.

EDGWORTH.

'Slight, he will call company, you shall see, and put us into doings presently.

165–166. *mallanders . . . quitter bone*] all diseases of the legs and feet in horses.

169–170. *Hospital*] St. Bartholomew's, overlooking the Fair.

172. *windgall*] a tumor on either side of a horse's leg.

172–173. *white of an egg . . . grease*] Knockem prescribes professional remedies; cf. Markham, pp. 366, 401.

176.1. *Exeunt . . . Ursula*] E.A.H. suggests that Ursula moves to the inner stage where the curtain may be drawn to form the backside of her booth (cf. II.vi.40–41).

JUSTICE OVERDO.

Thirst not after that frothy liquor, ale: for who knows, when he openeth the stopple, what may be in the bottle? Hath not a snail, a spider, yea, a newt been found there? Thirst not after it, youth; thirst not after it.

COKES.

This is a brave fellow, Numps, let's hear him.

WASP.

'Sblood, how brave is he? In a guarded coat? You were best truck with him; e'en strip, and truck presently, it will become you. Why will you hear him? Because he is an ass, and may be akin to the Cokeses?

COKES.

O, good Numps!

JUSTICE OVERDO.

Neither do thou lust after that tawny weed, tobacco.

COKES.

Brave words!

JUSTICE OVERDO.

Whose complexion is like the Indian's that vents it!

COKES.

Are they not brave words, sister?

JUSTICE OVERDO.

And who can tell if, before the gathering and making up thereof, the alligarta hath not piss'd thereon?

WASP.

'Heart, let 'em be brave words, as brave as they will! And they were all the brave words in a country, how then? Will you away yet? Ha' you enough on him? Mistress Grace, come you away, I pray you, be not you accessary. If you do lose your license, or somewhat else, sir, with list'ning to his fables, say Numps is a witch, with all my heart, do, say so.

COKES.

Avoid, i' your satin doublet, Numps.

---

16. *truck*] deal.
16. *strip*] move quickly (cf. outstrip).
22. *vents*] discharges.
25. *alligarta*] alligator.
31. *witch*] magician.
33. *avoid*] be off.

JUSTICE OVERDO.

The creeping venom of which subtle serpent, as some late writers affirm, neither the cutting of the perilous plant, nor the drying of it, nor the lighting, or burning, can any way persway or assuage.

COKES.

Good, i' faith! is't not, sister?

JUSTICE OVERDO.

Hence it is, that the lungs of the tobacconist are rotted, the liver spotted, the brain smok'd like the backside of the pig-woman's booth, here, and the whole body within, black as her pan you saw e'en now, without.

COKES.

A fine similitude, that, sir! Did you see the pan?

EDGWORTH.

Yes, sir.

JUSTICE OVERDO.

Nay, the hole in the nose here, of some tobacco-takers, or the third nostril (if I may so call it), which makes that they can vent the tobacco out like the ace of clubs, or rather the flower-de-lys, is caused from the tobacco, the mere tobacco! when the poor innocent pox, having nothing to do there, is miserably, and most unconscionably slander'd.

COKES.

Who would ha' miss'd this, sister?

MRS. OVERDO.

Not anybody, but Numps.

COKES.

He does not understand.

EDGWORTH.

Nor you feel. *He picketh his purse.*

COKES.

What would you have, sister, of a fellow that knows noth-

34–35. *some late writers*] James I wrote *A Counterblaste to Tobacco* in 1604.

37. *persway*] lessen.

39. *tobacconist*] smoker.

ing but a basket-hilt, and an old fox in't? The best music i' the Fair will not move a log.

EDGWORTH.

In, to Urs'la, Nightingale, and carry her comfort: see it told. This fellow was sent to us by fortune for our first fairing. [*Exit* Nightingale.]

JUSTICE OVERDO.

But what speak I of the diseases of the body, children of the Fair?

COKES.

That's to us, sister. Brave i' faith!

JUSTICE OVERDO.

Hark, O you sons and daughters of Smithfield! and hear what malady it doth the mind: it causeth swearing, it causeth swaggering, it causeth snuffling, and snarling, and now and then a hurt.

MRS. OVERDO.

He hath something of Master Overdo, methinks, brother.

COKES.

So methought, sister, very much of my brother Overdo: and 'tis when he speaks.

JUSTICE OVERDO.

Look into any angle o' the town (the Straits, or the Bermudas) where the quarreling lesson is read, and how do they entertain the time, but with bottle-ale, and tobacco? The lecturer is o' one side, and his pupils o' the other; but the seconds are still bottle-ale, and tobacco, for which the lecturer reads, and the novices pay. Thirty pound a week in bottle-ale! forty in tobacco! and ten more in ale again. Then for a suit to drink in, so much, and (that being slaver'd) so much for another suit, and then a third suit, and a fourth suit! and still the bottle-ale slavereth, and the tobacco stinketh!

---

57. *fox*] sword.

72–73. *Straits . . . Bermudas*] Jacobean names for streets and alleys near St. Martin's Lane where thieves and whores lived.

76. *seconds*] things which assist.

WASP.

Heart of a madman! are you rooted here? Will you never away? What can any man find out in this bawling fellow, to grow here for? He is a full handful higher, sin' he heard him. Will you fix here? And set up a booth? Sir?

JUSTICE OVERDO.

I will conclude briefly—

WASP.

Hold your peace, you roaring rascal, I'll run my head i' your chaps else. You were best build a booth, and entertain him, make your will, and you say the word, and him your heir! Heart, I never knew one taken with a mouth of a peck, afore. By this light, I'll carry you away o' my back, and you will not come.

He gets him up on pick-pack.

COKES.

Stay, Numps, stay, set me down: I ha' lost my purse, Numps, O my purse! One o' my fine purses is gone.

MRS. OVERDO.

Is't indeed, brother?

COKES.

Aye, as I am an honest man, would I were an arrant rogue, else! A plague of all roguy, damn'd cutpurses for me.

WASP.

Bless 'em with all my heart, with all my heart, do you see! Now, as I am no infidel, that I know of, I am glad on't. Aye I am; here's my witness! do you see, sir! I did not tell you of his fables, I? No, no, I am a dull malt-horse, I, I know nothing. Are you not justly serv'd i' your conscience now? Speak i' your conscience. Much good do you with all my heart, and his good heart that has it, with all my heart again.

EDGWORTH [*aside*].

This fellow is very charitable; would he had a purse too!

83. Will] F_3; well *F*.

92. *of a peck*] of two gallons' capacity.

93.1. *pick-pack*] pick-a-back. 103. *malt-horse*] dray-horse.

But I must not be too bold all at a time.

COKES.

Nay, Numps, it is not my best purse.

WASP.

Not your best! Death! why should it be your worst? Why should it be any, indeed, at all? Answer me to that, gi' me a reason from you, why it should be any?

COKES.

Nor my gold, Numps; I ha' that yet; look here else, sister.

WASP.

Why so, there's all the feeling he has!

MRS. OVERDO.

I pray you, have a better care of that, brother.

COKES.

Nay, so I will, I warrant you; let him catch this, that catch can. I would fain see him get this, look you here.

WASP.

So, so, so, so, so, so, so, so! Very good.

COKES.

I would ha' him come again, now, and but offer at it. Sister, will you take notice of a good jest? I will put it just where th' other was, and if we ha' good luck, you shall see a delicate fine trap to catch the cutpurse, nibbling.

EDGWORTH [*aside*].

Faith, and he'll try ere you be out o' the Fair.

COKES.

Come, Mistress Grace, prithee be not melancholy for my mischance; sorrow wi' not keep it, sweetheart.

GRACE.

I do not think on't sir.

COKES.

'Twas but a little scurvy white money, hang it: it may hang the cutpurse, one day. I ha' gold left to gi' thee a fairing, yet, as hard as the world goes: nothing angers me, but that nobody here look'd like a cutpurse, unless 'twere Numps.

WASP.

How? I? I look like a cutpurse? Death! your sister's a

129. *white money*] silver.

cutpurse! and your mother and father and all your kin were cutpurses! And here is a rogue is the bawd o' the cutpurses, whom I will beat to begin with.

They speak all together; and Wasp *beats the* Justice.

JUSTICE OVERDO.

Hold thy hand, child of wrath, and heir of anger, make it not Childermass day in thy fury, or the feast of the French Bartholomew, parent of the Massacre.

COKES.

Numps, Numps!

MRS. OVERDO.

Good Master Humphrey.

WASP.

You are the Patrico! are you? the patriarch of the cutpurses? You share, sir, they say, let them share this with you. Are you i' your hot fit of preaching again? I'll cool you.

JUSTICE OVERDO.

Murder, murder, murder! [*Exeunt.*]

[III.i] [*Enter*] Whit, Haggis, Bristle, Leatherhead, Trash.

WHIT.

Nay, 'tish all gone, now! Dish 'tish phen tou vilt not be phitin call, Mashter Offisher! Phat ish a man te better to lishen out noishes for tee and tou art in an oder 'orld—being very shuffishient noishes and gallantsh too, one o' their brabblesh would have fed ush all dish fortnight; but tou art so bushy about beggersh still, tou hast no leishure to intend shentlemen, and't be.

HAGGIS.

Why, I told you, Davy Bristle.

---

138. *Childermass*] the festival of the Innocents (December 28).
139. *French Bartholomew*] massacre of August 24, 1572.
142. *Patrico*] parson of the gypsies.

[III.i]

1–7] Whit speaks Elizabethan stage-Irish.
5. *brabblesh*] brabbles, noisy quarrels.

BRISTLE.

Come, come, you told me a pudding, Toby Haggis; a matter of nothing; I am sure it came to nothing! You said, "Let's go to Urs'la's," indeed; but then you met the man with the monsters, and I could not get you from him. An old fool, not leave seeing yet?

HAGGIS.

Why, who would ha' thought anybody would ha' quarrel'd so early? Or that the ale o' the Fair would ha' been up so soon?

WHIT.

Phy, phat a clock tost tou tink it ish, man?

HAGGIS.

I cannot tell.

WHIT.

Tou art a vishe vatchman, i' te mean teeme.

HAGGIS.

Why, should the watch go by the clock, or the clock by the watch, I pray?

BRISTLE.

One should go by another, if they did well.

WHIT.

Tou art right now! phen didst tou ever know or hear of a shuffishient vatchman but he did tell the clock, phat bushiness soever he had?

BRISTLE.

Nay, that's most true, a sufficient watchman knows what o'clock it is.

WHIT.

Shleeping, or vaking! ash well as te clock himshelf, or te jack dat shtrikes him!

BRISTLE.

Let's inquire of Master Leatherhead, or Joan Trash here. Master Leatherhead, do you hear, Master Leatherhead?

WHIT.

If it be a Ledderhead, tish a very tick Ledderhead, tat sho mush noish vill not peirsh him.

---

29. *jack*] figure which strikes the bell.

LEATHERHEAD.

I have a little business now; good friends, do not trouble me.

WHIT.

Phat? Because o' ty wrought neet-cap, and ty phelvet sherkin, man? Phy? I have sheen tee in ty ledder sherkin, ere now, mashter o' de hobbyhorses, as bushy and as stately as tou sheem'st to be.

TRASH.

Why, what an' you have, Captain Whit? He has his choice of jerkins, you may see by that, and his caps, too, I assure you, when he pleases to be either sick, or employ'd.

LEATHERHEAD.

God a mercy, Joan, answer for me.

WHIT.

Away, be not sheen i' my company; here be shentlemen, and men of vorship. [*Exeunt* Haggis, Bristle.]

[III.ii] [*Enter to them*] Quarlous, Winwife.

QUARLOUS.

We had wonderful ill luck to miss this prologue o' the purse, but the best is we shall have five acts of him ere night: he'll be spectacle enough! I'll answer for't.

WHIT.

O Creesh! Duke Quarlous, how dosht tou? Tou dosht not know me, I fear? I am te vishesht man, but Justish Overdo, in all Bartholomew Fair, now. Gi' me twelvepence from tee, I vill help tee to a vife vorth forty marks for't, an't be.

QUARLOUS.

Away, rogue, pimp, away.

WHIT.

And she shall show tee as fine cut 'ork for't in her shmock too, as tou cansht vish i' faith; vilt tou have her, vorshipful Vinvife? I vill help tee to her, here, be an't be, in te pig-quarter, gi' me ty twel'pence from tee.

[III.ii]

10. *cut 'ork*] cut work—lace or open-work embroidery, often worn by high-class prostitutes (cf. IV.vi.18–19).

WINWIFE.

Why, there's twel'pence; pray thee, wilt thou be gone?

WHIT.

Tou art a vorthy man, and a vorshipful man still.

QUARLOUS.

Get you gone, rascal.

WHIT.

I do mean it, man. Prinsh Quarlous, if tou hasht need on me, tou shalt find me here, at Urs'la's; I vill see phat ale and punk ish i' te pigshty for tee, bless ty good vorship. [*Exit.*]

QUARLOUS.

Look! who comes here! John Littlewit!

WINWIFE.

And his wife, and my widow, her mother: the whole family.

QUARLOUS.

'Slight, you must gi' em all fairings, now!

WINWIFE.

Not I, I'll not see 'em.

QUARLOUS.

They are going a-feasting. What schoolmaster's that is with 'em?

WINWIFE.

That's my rival, I believe, the baker!

[*Enter*] Busy, Purecraft, Littlewit, Win.

BUSY.

So, walk on in the middle way, fore-right, turn neither to the right hand, nor to the left: let not your eyes be drawn aside with vanity, nor your ear with noises.

QUARLOUS.

O, I know him by that start!

LEATHERHEAD.

What do you lack? What do you buy, pretty mistress! a fine hobbyhorse, to make your son a tilter? a drum to make him a soldier? a fiddle, to make him a reveler?

---

28. *fore-right*] straight ahead.
33. *tilter*] jouster.

What is't you lack? Little dogs for your daughters! or babies, male, or female?

BUSY.

Look not toward them, hearken not: the place is Smithfield, or the field of smiths, the grove of hobbyhorses and trinkets, the wares are the wares of devils. And the whole Fair is the shop of Satan! They are hooks, and baits, very baits, that are hung out on every side, to catch you, and to hold you as it were, by the gills, and by the nostrils, as the fisher doth: therefore, you must not look, nor turn toward them—the heathen man could stop his ears with wax, against the harlot o' the sea: do you the like, with your fingers, against the bells of the Beast.

WINWIFE.

What flashes comes from him!

QUARLOUS.

O, he has those of his oven! A notable hot baker 'twas, when he plied the peel: he is leading his flock into the Fair, now.

WINWIFE.

Rather driving 'em to the pens: for he will let 'em look upon nothing.

[*Enter*] Knockem, Whit.

KNOCKEM.

Gentlewomen, the weather's hot! Whither walk you? Have a care o' your fine velvet caps; the Fair is dusty. Take a sweet delicate booth, with boughs, here, i' the way, and cool yourselves i' the shade: you and your friends. The best pig and bottle-ale i' the Fair, sir. Old Urs'la is cook, there you may read: the pig's head speaks it.

Littlewit *is gazing at the sign; which is the Pig's Head with a large writing under it.*

---

44. *heathen-man*] Ulysses; but, characteristically Busy's classical allusion is somewhat wrong.

49. *peel*] shovel for handling loaves.

55. *delicate*] delightful.

Poor soul, she has had a stringhalt, the maryhinchco: but she's prettily amended.

WHIT.

A delicate show-pig, little mistress, with shweet sauce, and crackling, like de bay-leaf i' de fire, la! Tou shalt ha' de clean side o' de table-clot and dy glass vash'd with phatersh of Dame Annessh Cleare. [*Exit.*]

LITTLEWIT.

This's fine, verily; "Here be the best pigs, and she does roast 'em as well as ever she did," the pig's head says.

KNOCKEM.

Excellent, excellent, mistress, with fire o' juniper and rosemary branches! The oracle of the pig's head, that, sir.

PURECRAFT.

Son, were you not warn'd of the vanity of the eye? Have you forgot the wholesome admonition, so soon?

LITTLEWIT.

Good mother, how shall we find a pig, if we do not look about for't? Will it run off o' the spit into our mouths, think you? as in Lubberland? and cry, "We, we"?

BUSY.

No, but your mother, religiously wise, conceiveth it may offer itself by other means to the sense, as by way of steam, which I think it doth, here in this place. Huh, huh —yes, it doth.

Busy *scents after it like a hound.*

And it were a sin of obstinacy, great obstinacy, high and horrible obstinacy, to decline, or resist the good titillation of the famelic sense, which is the smell. Therefore be bold (huh, huh, huh), follow the scent. Enter the tents of the unclean, for once, and satisfy your wife's frailty. Let

---

59. *stringhalt*] also called the maryhinchcho, a sudden twitching up of the horse's hind legs.

64. *Dame Annessh Cleare*] a spring named after a rich widow, Annis Clare.

67. *juniper*] burned to purify the air.

73. *Lubberland*] "where the pigs run about red, roasted, and cry, Come eat me" (Nares).

80. *famelic*] exciting hunger.

your frail wife be satisfied: your zealous mother, and my suffering self, will also be satisfied.

LITTLEWIT.

Come, Win, as good winny here as go farther and see nothing.

BUSY.

We 'scape so much of the other vanities, by our early ent'ring.

PURECRAFT.

It is an edifying consideration.

WIN.

This is scurvy, that we must come into the Fair and not look on't.

LITTLEWIT.

Win, have patience, Win, I'll tell you more anon.

KNOCKEM.

Mooncalf, entertain within there; the best pig i' the booth, a pork-like pig. These are Banbury-bloods, o' the sincere stud, come a pig-hunting. Whit, wait, Whit, look to your charge.

BUSY.

A pig prepare, presently, let a pig be prepared to us.

[*He leads off* Littlewit, Win, Purecraft.]

[*Enter*] Mooncalf, Ursula.

MOONCALF.

'Slight, who be these?

URSULA.

Is this the good service, Jordan, you'd do me?

KNOCKEM.

Why, Urs? Why, Urs? Thou'lt ha' vapors i' thy leg again presently; pray thee go in, 't may turn to the scratches else.

URSULA.

Hang your vapors, they are stale, and stink like you; are these the guests o' the game you promis'd to fill my pit withal, today?

---

85. *winny*] stay. 95. *sincere*] genuine. 95. *stud*] breed.
101. *scratches*] cf. II.v.166.

KNOCKEM.

Aye, what ail they, Urs?

URSULA.

Ail they? They are all sippers, sippers o' the city; they look as they would not drink off two penn'orth of bottle-ale amongst 'em.

MOONCALF.

A body may read that i' their small printed ruffs.

KNOCKEM.

Away, thou art a fool, Urs, and thy Mooncalf too, i' your ignorant vapors, now! hence, good guests, I say right hypocrites, good gluttons. In, and set a couple o' pigs o' the board, and half a dozen of the biggest bottles afore 'em, and call Whit. I do not love to hear innocents abus'd: fine ambling hypocrites! and a stone-puritan, with a sorrel head, and beard, good mouth'd gluttons: two to a pig, away. [*Exit* Mooncalf.]

URSULA.

Are you sure they are such?

KNOCKEM.

O' the right breed, thou shalt try 'em by the teeth, Urs. Where's this Whit?

[*Re-enter* Whit.]

WHIT.

Behold, man, and see, what a worthy man am ee!
With the fury of my sword, and the shaking of my beard,
I will make ten thousand men afeard.

KNOCKEM.

Well said, brave Whit; in, and fear the ale out o' the bottles into the bellies of the brethren, and the sisters; drink to the cause, and pure vapors.

[*Exeunt* Knockem, Whit, Ursula.]

QUARLOUS.

My roarer is turn'd tapster, methinks. Now were a fine time for thee, Winwife, to lay aboard thy widow; thou'lt

---

110. *small printed*] exactly folded in a small or Geneva print.
116. *stone-puritan*] lustful Puritan; cf. *stone-horse,* stallion.
117. *sorrel*] chestnut colored.
129. *lay aboard*] place one's ship alongside another for attack.

never be master of a better season, or place; she that will venture herself into the Fair, and a pig-box, will admit any assault, be assur'd of that.

WINWIFE.

I love not enterprises of that suddenness, though.

QUARLOUS.

I'll warrant thee, then, no wife out o' the widow's hundred: if I had but as much title to her, as to have breath'd once on that strait stomacher of hers, I would now assure myself to carry her, yet, ere she went out of Smithfield. Or she should carry me, which were the fitter sight, I confess. But you are a modest undertaker, by circumstances, and degrees; come, 'tis disease in thee, not judgment: I should offer at all together. Look, here's the poor fool again that was stung by the wasp, erewhile.

[III.iii] [*Enter*] Justice.

JUSTICE OVERDO.

I will make no more orations, shall draw on these tragical conclusions. And I begin now to think that, by a spice of collateral justice, Adam Overdo deserv'd this beating; for I, the said Adam, was one cause (a by-cause) why the purse was lost: and my wife's brother's purse too, which they know not of yet. But I shall make very good mirth with it, at supper (that will be the sport), and put my little friend Master Humphrey Wasp's choler quite out of countenance. When, sitting at the upper end o' my table, as I use, and drinking to my brother Cokes and Mistress Alice Overdo, as I will, my wife, for their good affection to old Bradley, I deliver to 'em it was I that was

---

134–135. *hundred*] subdivision of a county, having its own court.

136. *stomacher*] an ornamental covering for the chest worn under the bodice.

137. *carry*] win.

139. *undertaker*] one who takes up a challenge.

141. *offer at*] make an attempt at.

[III.iii]

3. *collateral*] accompanying.

4. *by-cause*] incidental cause.

cudgel'd and show 'em the marks. To see what bad events may peep out o' the tail of good purposes! The care I had of that civil young man I took fancy to this morning (and have not left it yet) drew me to that exhortation, which drew the company, indeed, which drew the cutpurse; which drew the money; which drew my brother Cokes his loss; which drew on Wasp's anger; which drew on my beating: a pretty gradation! And they shall ha' it i' their dish, i' faith, at night for fruit: I love to be merry at my table. I had thought once, at one special blow he ga' me, to have revealed myself! But then (I thank thee, fortitude) I remember'd that a wise man (and who is ever so great a part o' the Commonwealth in himself) for no particular disaster ought to abandon a public good design. The husbandman ought not, for one unthankful year, to forsake the plough; the shepherd ought not, for one scabb'd sheep, to throw by his tar-box; the pilot ought not, for one leak i' the poop, to quit the helm; nor the alderman ought not, for one custard more, at a meal, to give up his cloak; the constable ought not to break his staff, and forswear the watch, for one roaring night; nor the piper o' the parish (*ut parvis componere magna solebam*) to put up his pipes, for one rainy Sunday. These are certain knocking conclusions; out of which I am resolv'd, come what come can: come beating, come imprisonment, come infamy, come banishment, nay, come the rack, come the hurdle (welcome all), I will not discover who I am till my due time; and yet still all shall be, as I said ever, in Justice' name, and the King's, and for the Commonwealth!

WINWIFE.

What does he talk to himself, and act so seriously? Poor fool! [*Exit*] Justice.

QUARLOUS.

No matter what. Here's fresher argument, intend that.

29. *tar-box*] to hold tar-salve for sores in sheep.

34–35. *ut . . . solebam*] "*sic . . .*" in Virgil *Ecl.* I. 23: "thus I used to compare great things with small."

43. *What*] why.

45. *intend*] attend to.

[III.iv.] [*Enter to them*] Cokes, Mistress Overdo, Grace, Wasp.

COKES.
Come, Mistress Grace, come sister, here's more fine sights yet, i' faith. God's lid, where's Numps?

LEATHERHEAD.
What do you lack, gentlemen? What is't you buy? Fine rattles! Drums? Babies? Little dogs? And birds for ladies? What do you lack?

COKES.
Good honest Numps, keep afore, I am so afraid thou'lt lose somewhat: my heart was at my mouth when I miss'd thee.

WASP.
You were best buy a whip i' your hand to drive me.

COKES.
Nay, do not mistake, Numps, thou art so apt to mistake: I would but watch the goods. Look you now, the treble fiddle was e'en almost like to be lost.

WASP.
Pray you take heed you lose not yourself: your best way were e'en get up and ride for more surety. Buy a token's worth of great pins, to fasten yourself to my shoulder.

LEATHERHEAD.
What do you lack, gentlemen? Fine purses, pouches, pincases, pipes? What is't you lack? A pair o' smiths to wake you i' the morning? Or a fine whistling bird?

COKES.
Numps, here be finer things than any we ha' bought, by odds! And more delicate horses, a great deal! Good Numps, stay, and come hither.

WASP.
Will you scourse with him? You are in Smithfield, you may fit yourself with a fine easy-going street-nag for your saddle again' Michaelmas term, do; has he ne'er a little

---

17. *pair o' smiths*] "two pieces of beaten metal to form a bell (by hanging one up and striking it with the other)" (E.A.H.).

22. *scourse*] deal.

odd cart for you, to make a caroche on, i' the country, with four pied hobbyhorses? Why the measles, should you stand here, with your train, cheaping of dogs, birds, and babies? You ha' no children to bestow 'em on? Ha' you?

COKES.

No, but again' I ha' children, Numps, that's all one.

WASP.

Do, do, do, do; how many shall you have, think you? An' I were as you, I'd buy for all my tenants, too: they are a kind o' civil savages, that will part with their children for rattles, pipes, and knives. You were best buy a hatchet, or two, and truck with 'em.

COKES.

Good Numps, hold that little tongue o' thine, and save it a labor. I am resolute Bat, thou know'st.

WASP.

A resolute fool you are, I know, and a very sufficient coxcomb; with all my heart; nay, you have it, sir, and you be angry, turd i' your teeth, twice (if I said it not once afore): and much good do you.

WINWIFE.

Was there ever such a self-affliction? And so impertinent?

QUARLOUS.

Alas! his care will go near to crack him: let's in, and comfort him.

WASP.

Would I had been set i' the ground, all but the head on me, and had my brains bowl'd at, or thresh'd out, when first I underwent this plague of a charge!

QUARLOUS.

How now, Numps! Almost tir'd i' your protectorship? Overparted? Overparted?

---

25. *caroche*] a rich carriage.
27. *cheaping*] buying.
33. *civil*] civilized.
43. *crack*] craze.
49. *Overparted*] given too difficult a part.

WASP.

Why, I cannot tell, sir; it may be I am; does't grieve you?

QUARLOUS.

No, I swear does't not, Numps: to satisfy you.

WASP.

Numps? 'Sblood, you are fine and familiar! How long ha' we been acquainted, I pray you?

QUARLOUS.

I think it may be remember'd, Numps, that? 'Twas since morning sure.

WASP.

Why, I hope I know't well enough, sir; I did not ask to be told.

QUARLOUS.

No? Why then?

WASP.

It's no matter why; you see with your eyes, now, what I said to you today? You'll believe me another time?

QUARLOUS.

Are you removing the Fair, Numps?

WASP.

A pretty question! and a very civil one! Yes faith, I ha' my lading you see, or shall have anon; you may know whose beast I am by my burden. If the pannier-man's jack were ever better known by his loins of mutton, I'll be flay'd and feed dogs for him, when his time comes.

WINWIFE.

How melancholy Mistress Grace is yonder! Pray thee let's go enter ourselves in grace, with her.

COKES.

Those six horses, friend, I'll have—

WASP.

How!

COKES.

And the three Jew's trumps; and half a dozen o' birds,

---

64. *pannier-man*] servant in Inns of Court.
65. *jack*] laborer.
68. *grace*] favor.
71. *Jew's trumps*] Jew's harps.

and that drum (I have one drum already) and your smiths (I like that device o' your smiths, very pretty well) and four halberts—and (le' me see) that fine painted great lady, and her three women for state, I'll have.

WASP.

No, the shop; buy the whole shop, it will be best, the shop, the shop!

LEATHERHEAD.

If his worship please.

WASP.

Yes, and keep it during the Fair, bobchin.

COKES.

Peace, Numps. Friend, do not meddle with him, an' you be wise, and would show your head above board: he will sting through your wrought nightcap, believe me. A set of these violins I would buy too, for a delicate young noise I have i' the country, that are every one a size less than another, just like your fiddles. I would fain have a fine young masque at my marriage, now I think on't: but I do want such a number o' things. And Numps will not help me now, and I dare not speak to him.

TRASH.

Will your worship buy any gingerbread, very good bread, comfortable bread?

COKES.

Gingerbread! Yes, let's see. *He runs to her shop.*

WASP.

There's the tother springe!

LEATHERHEAD.

Is this well, goody Joan? To interrupt my market? In the midst? And call away my customers? Can you answer this, at the Pie-powders?

TRASH.

Why? if his mastership have a mind to buy, I hope my

---

75. *state*] splendor.
79. *bobchin*] apparently, fool (whose chin jerks up and down).
81. *above board*] in sight of all.
84. *noise*] band of musicians.
86. *masque*] a group of masquers.
92. *springe*] snare.

ware lies as open as another's; I may show my ware, as well as you yours.

COKES.

Hold your peace; I'll content you both: I'll buy up his shop, and thy basket.

WASP.

Will you i' faith?

LEATHERHEAD.

Why should you put him from it, friend?

WASP.

Cry you mercy! you'd be sold too, would you? What's the price on you? Jerkin, and all as you stand? Ha' you any qualities?

TRASH.

Yes, Goodman Angry-man, you shall find he has qualities, if you cheapen him.

WASP.

Godso, you ha' the selling of him! What are they? Will they be bought for love, or money?

TRASH.

No indeed, sir.

WASP.

For what then? Victuals?

TRASH.

He scorns victuals, sir; he has bread and butter at home, thanks be to God! And yet he will do more for a good meal, if the toy take him i' the belly; marry then they must not set him at lower end; if they do, he'll go away, though he fast. But put him atop o' the table, where his place is, and he'll do you forty fine things. He has not been sent for, and sought out, for nothing, at your great city-suppers, to put down Coriat, and Cokely, and been

---

105. *qualities*] accomplishments.

107. *cheapen*] ask the price of.

108. *Godso*] sometimes *Catso,* from Italian *cazzo,* penis.

116. *atop o' the table*] the jester's place.

119. *Coriat*] Thomas Coryat, jester to Prince Henry and author of *Coryat's Crudities* (1611).

119. *Cokely*] another famous jester; cf. *Ep.* CXXIX, 16–17.

laugh'd at for his labor; he'll play you all the puppets i' the town over, and the players, every company, and his own company too; he spares nobody!

COKES.

I' faith?

TRASH.

He was the first, sir, that ever baited the fellow i' the bear's skin, an't like your worship: no dog ever came near him, since. And for fine motions!

COKES.

Is he good at those too? Can he set out a masque, trow?

TRASH.

O Lord, Master! sought to, far and near, for his inventions: and he engrosses all, he makes all the puppets i' the Fair.

COKES.

Dost thou (in troth), old velvet jerkin? Give me thy hand.

TRASH.

Nay, sir, you shall see him in his velvet jerkin, and a scarf, too, at night, when you hear him interpret Master Littlewit's motion.

COKES.

Speak no more, but shut up shop presently, friend. I'll buy both it and thee too, to carry down with me, and her hamper, beside. Thy shop shall furnish out the masque, and hers the banquet: I cannot go less, to set out anything with credit. What's the price, at a word, o' thy whole shop, case and all as it stands?

LEATHERHEAD.

Sir, it stands me in six and twenty shillings sevenpence halfpenny, besides three shillings for my ground.

124–125. *fellow . . . skin*] apparently an actor at the Fortune who put on a bear's skin and was nearly killed in the subsequent baiting.

126. *motions*] puppet-shows.

127. *trow?*] do you suppose?

129. *engrosses*] monopolizes the trade.

139. *banquet*] here, dessert.

142. *stands me in*] costs.

COKES.

Well, thirty shillings will do all, then! And what comes yours to?

TRASH.

Four shillings and elevenpence, sir, ground and all, an't like your worship.

COKES.

Yes, it does like my worship very well; poor woman, that's five shillings more. What a masque shall I furnish out for forty shillings (twenty pound Scotch)! And a banquet of gingerbread! There's a stately thing! Numps! Sister! And my wedding gloves too! (That I never thought on afore.) All my wedding gloves, gingerbread! O me! what a device will there be, to make 'em eat their fingers' ends! And delicate brooches for the bridemen! And all! And then I'll ha' this posy put to 'em: "For the best grace," meaning Mistress Grace, my wedding posy.

GRACE.

I am beholden to you, sir, and to your Bartholomew-wit.

WASP.

You do not mean this, do you? Is this your first purchase?

COKES.

Yes, faith, and I do not think, Numps, but thou'lt say, it was the wisest act, that ever I did in my wardship.

WASP.

Like enough! I shall say anything. I!

[III.v] [*Enter to them*] Justice, Edgworth, Nightingale.

JUSTICE OVERDO [*aside*].

I cannot beget a project, with all my political brain, yet; my project is how to fetch off this proper young man from his debauch'd company: I have followed him all the Fair over, and still I find him with this songster; and I

145. to] *1716*; too *F*.

---

150. *pound Scotch*] 1*s*. 8*d*. sterling.

156. *posy*] motto.

[III.v]

1. *political*] shrewd.

begin shrewdly to suspect their familiarity; and the young man of a terrible taint, poetry! with which idle disease if he be infected, there's no hope of him, in a state-course. *Actum est* of him for a commonwealths-man, if he go to't in rhyme once.

EDGWORTH [*to Nightingale*].

Yonder he is buying o' gingerbread: set in quickly, before he part with too much on his money.

NIGHTINGALE.

My masters and friends, and good people, draw near, &c.

COKES.

Ballads! hark, hark! Pray thee, fellow, stay a little; good Numps, look to the goods. What ballads hast thou? Let me see, let me see myself.

He runs to the ballad-man.

WASP.

Why so! he's flown to another lime-bush; there he will flutter as long more, till he ha' ne'er a feather left. Is there a vexation like this, gentlemen? Will you believe me now, hereafter? Shall I have credit with you?

QUARLOUS.

Yes faith, shalt thou, Numps, and thou art worthy on't, for thou sweatest for't. I never saw a young pimp errant and his squire better match'd.

WINWIFE.

Faith, the sister comes after 'em, well, too.

GRACE.

Nay, if you saw the Justice her husband, my guardian, you were fitted for the mess; he is such a wise one his way—

WINWIFE.

I wonder we see him not here.

---

7. *state-course*] career in public service?
8. *Actum . . . him*] "It's all over with him."
8. *commonwealths-man*] good citizen.
16. *lime-bush*] snare (bush smeared with birdlime).
25. *mess*] a set of four (originally a group into which a banqueting company was divided).

GRACE.

O! he is too serious for this place, and yet better sport than the other three, I assure you, gentlemen: where'er he is, though't be o' the bench.

COKES.

How dost thou call it? *A caveat against cutpurses!* a good jest, i' faith; I would fain see that demon, your cutpurse, you talk of, that delicate-handed devil; they say he walks hereabout: I would see him walk, now. Look you, sister, here, here, let him come, sister, and welcome.

He shows his purse boastingly.

Ballad-man, does any cutpurses haunt hereabout? Pray thee raise me one or two: begin and show me one.

NIGHTINGALE.

Sir, this is a spell against 'em, spick and span new; and 'tis made as 'twere in mine own person, and I sing it in mine own defense. But 'twill cost a penny alone, if you buy it.

COKES.

No matter for the price; thou dost not know me, I see; I am an odd Bartholomew.

MRS. OVERDO.

Has't a fine picture, brother?

COKES.

O sister, do you remember the ballads over the nursery-chimney at home o' my own pasting up? There be brave pictures. Other manner of pictures, than these, friend.

WASP.

Yet these will serve to pick the pictures out o' your pockets, you shall see.

COKES.

So I heard 'em say. Pray thee mind him not, fellow: he'll have an oar in everything.

NIGHTINGALE.

It was intended, sir, as if a purse should chance to be cut in my presence, now, I may be blameless, though: as by

29. than] then then *F.*

48. *pictures*] the king's pictures on coins.

the sequel, will more plainly appear.

COKES.

We shall find that i' the matter. Pray thee begin.

NIGHTINGALE.

To the tune of *Paggington's Pound,* sir.

COKES.

Fa, la la la, la la la, fa la la la. Nay, I'll put thee in tune, and all! Mine own country dance! Pray thee begin.

NIGHTINGALE.

It is a gentle admonition, you must know, sir, both to the purse-cutter, and the purse-bearer.

COKES.

Not a word more, out o' the tune, an' thou lov'st me: Fa, la la la, la la la, fa la la la. Come, when?

NIGHTINGALE.

My masters and friends and good people draw near,
And look to your purses, for that I do say;

COKES.

Ha, ha, this chimes! Good counsel at first dash.

NIGHTINGALE.

And though little money, in them you do bear,
It cost more to get, than to lose in a day.

COKES.

Good!

NIGHTINGALE.

You oft have been told,
Both the young and the old;
And bidden beware of the cutpurse so bold;

COKES.

Well said! He were to blame that would not, i' faith.

NIGHTINGALE.

Then if you take heed not, free me from the curse,
Who both give you warning, for and the cutpurse.
Youth, youth, thou hadst better been starv'd by thy nurse,

68. *During this scene in which Cokes's pocket is picked (l. 68 to l. 164) a number of speeches of Cokes, two of Winwife, and one of Quarlous are placed on the right-hand column of the Folio to indicate that they are said while Nightingale is singing. Here they have been added between the lines of the song.*

74. *for and*] and also.

Than live to be hanged for cutting a purse.

COKES.

Good i' faith, how say you, Numps? Is there any harm i' this?

NIGHTINGALE.

It hath been upbraided to men of my trade,
That oftentimes we are the cause of this crime.

COKES.

The more coxcombs they that did it, I wusse.

NIGHTINGALE.

Alack and for pity, why should it be said?
As if they regarded or places, or time.
Examples have been
Of some that were seen,
In Westminster Hall, yea the pleaders between,
Then why should the judges be free from this curse,
More than my poor self, for cutting the purse?

COKES.

God a mercy for that! Why should they be more free indeed?

NIGHTINGALE.

Youth, youth, thou hadst better been starv'd by thy nurse,
Than live to be hanged for cutting a purse.

COKES.

That again, good ballad-man, that again.

He sings the burden with him.

O rare! I would fain rub mine elbow now, but I dare not pull out my hand. On, I pray thee; he that made this ballad shall be poet to my masque.

NIGHTINGALE.

At Worc'ster, 'tis known well, and even i' the jail,
A knight of good worship did there show his face,
Against the foul sinners, in zeal for to rail,
And lost (ipso facto) *his purse in the place.*

COKES.

Is it possible?

---

86. *Westminster Hall*] Courts of Common Law and of Chancery sat in the great hall of the Palace until the late eighteenth century.

94. *rub mine elbow*] show pleasure.

NIGHTINGALE.

Nay, once from the seat
Of judgment so great,
A judge there did lose a fair pouch of velvet.

COKES.

I' faith?

NIGHTINGALE.

O Lord for thy mercy, how wicked or worse
Are those that so venture their necks for a purse!
Youth, youth, &c.

COKES. *Youth, youth, &c.*

Pray thee stay a little, friend; yet o' thy conscience, Numps, speak, is there any harm i' this?

WASP.

To tell you true, 'tis too good for you, 'less you had grace to follow it.

JUSTICE OVERDO [*aside*].

It doth discover enormity, I'll mark it more: I ha' not lik'd a paltry piece of poetry so well, a good while.

COKES. *Youth, youth, &c.*

Where's this youth, now? A man must call upon him, for his own good, and yet he will not appear: look here, here's for him; handy-dandy, which hand will he have?

He shows his purse.

On, I pray thee, with the rest; I do hear of him, but I cannot see him, this Master Youth, the cutpurse.

NIGHTINGALE.

At plays and at sermons, and at the sessions,
'Tis daily their practice such booty to make:
Yea, under the gallows, at executions,
They stick not the stare-abouts' purses to take.
Nay, one without grace,
At a far better place,

127. *far*] *G. conj.; not in F.*

---

104. *judge . . . velvet*] an allusion to a similar trick played by Sir Thomas More on a justice at Newgate.

119. *handy-dandy*] a game of guessing which hand contains a concealed object.

At court, and in Christmas, before the King's face.

COKES.

That was a fine fellow! I would have him, now.

NIGHTINGALE.

Alack then for pity, must I bear the curse,
That only belongs to the cunning cutpurse?

COKES.

But where's their cunning, now, when they should use it?
They are all chain'd now, I warrant you.

Youth, youth, thou hadst better, &c.

The rat-catcher's charm, are all fools and asses to this? A pox on 'em, that they will not come! that a man should have such a desire to a thing, and want it.

QUARLOUS.

'Fore God, I'd give half the Fair, and 'twere mine, for a cutpurse for him, to save his longing.

COKES.

Look you, sister, here, here, where is't now? which pocket is't in, for a wager?

He shows his purse again.

WASP.

I beseech you leave your wagers, and let him end his matter, an't may be.

COKES.

O, are you edified, Numps?

JUSTICE OVERDO [*aside*].

Indeed he does interrupt him, too much: there Numps spoke to purpose.

COKES.

Sister, I am an ass, I cannot keep my purse.

[*He shows it*] *again.*

135. this?] *E.A.H.*; this! *F.*

---

128. *At . . . King's face*] John Selman was executed in January, 1612, for having done precisely this; cf. H.S., X, 200.

135. *rat-catcher's charm*] in apposition to "this" (E.A.H.); Cokes thinks he can charm pickpockets by his singing, almost as the Pied Piper did the rats of Hamelin; also proverbially rats could be rhymed to death in Ireland.

On, on; I pray thee, friend.

WINWIFE.

Will you see sport? look, there's a fellow gathers up to him, mark.

Edgworth *gets up to him and tickles him in the ear with a straw twice to draw his hand out of his pocket.*

QUARLOUS.

Good, i' faith! O, he has lighted on the wrong pocket.

WINWIFE.

He has it, 'fore God, he is a brave fellow; pity he should be detected.

NIGHTINGALE.

But O, you vile nation of cutpurses all,
Relent and repent, and amend and be sound,
And know that you ought not, by honest men's fall,
Advance your own fortunes, to die above ground,
And though you go gay,
In silks as you may,
It is not the high way to heaven (as they say).
Repent then, repent you, for better, for worse:
And kiss not the gallows for cutting a purse.
Youth, youth, thou hadst better been starv'd by thy nurse,
Than live to be hanged for cutting a purse.

ALL.

An excellent ballad! an excellent ballad!

EDGWORTH.

Friend, let me ha' the first, let me ha' the first, I pray you.

COKES.

Pardon me, sir. First come, first serv'd; and I'll buy the whole bundle too.

WINWIFE.

That conveyance was better than all, did you see't? He has given the purse to the ballad-singer.

152–153. God . . . detected.] *F, between ll. 164 and 165.*

---

149. *gathers*] draws?

QUARLOUS.

Has he?

EDGWORTH.

Sir, I cry you mercy; I'll not hinder the poor man's profit: pray you, mistake me not.

COKES.

Sir, I take you for an honest gentleman, if that be mistaking; I met you today afore: ha! humh! O God! my purse is gone, my purse, my purse, &c.

WASP.

Come, do not make a stir, and cry yourself an ass through the Fair afore your time.

COKES.

Why, hast thou it, Numps? Good Numps, how came you by it? I mar'l!

WASP.

I pray you seek some other gamester to play the fool with: you may lose it time enough, for all your Fair-wit.

COKES.

By this good hand, glove and all, I ha' lost it already, if thou hast it not: feel else, and Mistress Grace's handkercher, too, out o' the tother pocket.

WASP.

Why, 'tis well; very well, exceeding pretty, and well.

EDGWORTH.

Are you sure you ha' lost it, sir?

COKES.

O God! yes; as I am an honest man, I had it but e'en now, at "Youth, youth."

NIGHTINGALE.

I hope you suspect not me, sir.

EDGWORTH.

Thee? that were a jest indeed! Dost thou think the gentleman is foolish? Where hadst thou hands, I pray thee? Away, ass, away. [*Exit* Nightingale.]

JUSTICE OVERDO [*aside*].

I shall be beaten again, if I be spied.

---

180. *marl*] marvel.

184–185. *handkercher*] handkerchief.

EDGWORTH.

Sir, I suspect an odd fellow, yonder, is stealing away.

MRS. OVERDO.

Brother, it is the preaching fellow! You shall suspect him. He was at your tother purse, you know! Nay, stay, sir, and view the work you ha' done; an' you be benefic'd at the gallows, and preach there, thank your own handiwork.

COKES.

Sir, you shall take no pride in your preferment: you shall be silenc'd quickly.

JUSTICE OVERDO.

What do you mean, sweet buds of gentility?

COKES.

To ha' my pennyworths out on you: bud! No less than two purses a day, serve you? I thought you a simple fellow, when my man Numps beat you, i' the morning, and pitied you—

MRS. OVERDO.

So did I, I'll be sworn, brother; but now I see he is a lewd, and pernicious enormity (as Master Overdo calls him).

JUSTICE OVERDO [*aside*].

Mine own words turn'd upon me, like swords.

COKES.

Cannot a man's purse be at quiet for you, i' the master's pocket, but you must entice it forth, and debauch it?

[Justice Overdo *is carried off*.]

WASP.

Sir, sir, keep your debauch and your fine Bartholomew-terms to yourself; and make as much on 'em as you please. But gi' me this from you, i' the meantime: I beseech you, see if I can look to this. Wasp *takes the license from him.*

COKES.

Why, Numps?

WASP.

Why? because you are an ass, sir, there's a reason the

196. *suspect*] take note of.

213. *entice . . . debauch*] Wasp calls these "fine . . . terms" because the distinction between them is very slight.

shortest way, and you will needs ha' it; now you ha' got the trick of losing, you'd lose your breech, an't 'twere loose. I know you, sir, come, deliver, you'll go and crack the vermin you breed now, will you? 'Tis very fine, will you ha' the truth on't? They are such retchless flies as you are, that blow cutpurses abroad in every corner; your foolish having of money makes 'em. An' there were no wiser than I, sir, the trade should lie open for you, sir, it should i' faith, sir. I would teach your wit to come to your head, sir, as well as your land to come into your hand, I assure you, sir.

WINWIFE.

Alack, good Numps.

WASP.

Nay, gentlemen, never pity me, I am not worth it: Lord send me at home once, to Harrow o' the Hill again, if I travel any more, call me Coriat; with all my heart.

[*Exeunt* Wasp, Cokes *and* Mistress Overdo.]

QUARLOUS.

Stay, sir, I must have a word with you in private. Do you hear?

EDGWORTH.

With me, sir? What's your pleasure, good sir?

QUARLOUS.

Do not deny it. You are a cutpurse, sir; this gentleman here, and I, saw you, nor do we mean to detect you, though we can sufficiently inform ourselves, toward the danger of concealing you; but you must do us a piece of service.

EDGWORTH.

Good gentlemen, do not undo me; I am a civil young man, and but a beginner, indeed.

QUARLOUS.

Sir, your beginning shall bring on your ending, for us. We are no catchpoles nor constables. That you are to undertake, is this: you saw the old fellow, with the black box, here?

---

224. *retchless*] careless.
246. *catchpoles*] sheriff's officers.

EDGWORTH.

The little old governor, sir?

QUARLOUS.

That same: I see, you have flown him to a mark already. I would ha' you get away that box from him, and bring it us.

EDGWORTH.

Would you ha' the box and all, sir? or only that, that is in't? I'll get you that, and leave him the box to play with still (which will be the harder o' the two), because I would gain your worship's good opinion of me.

WINWIFE.

He says well, 'tis the greater mast'ry, and 'twill make the more sport when 'tis miss'd.

EDGWORTH.

Aye, and 'twill be the longer a-missing, to draw on the sport.

QUARLOUS.

But look you do it now, sirrah, and keep your word: or—

EDGWORTH.

Sir, if ever I break my word, with a gentleman, may I never read word at my need. Where shall I find you?

QUARLOUS.

Somewhere i' the Fair, hereabouts. Dispatch it quickly.

[*Exit* Edgworth.]

—I would fain see the careful fool deluded! Of all beasts, I love the serious ass: he that takes pains to be one, and plays the fool, with the greatest diligence that can be.

GRACE.

Then you would not choose, sir, but love my guardian, Justice Overdo, who is answerable to that description, in every hair of him.

QUARLOUS.

So I have heard. But how came you, Mistress Wellborn, to be his ward, or have relation to him, at first?

266. ass:] *E.A.H.*; Asse. *F.*

---

249. *governor*] tutor.
263. *read word*] cf. I.iv.6–7, and note.

GRACE.

Faith, through a common calamity, he bought me, sir; and now he will marry me to his wife's brother, this wise gentleman, that you see, or else I must pay value o' my land.

QUARLOUS.

'Slid, is there no device of disparagement, or so? Talk with some crafty fellow, some picklock o' the Law! Would I had studied a year longer i' the Inns of Court, and't had been but i' your case.

WINWIFE (*aside*).

Aye, Master Quarlous, are you proffering?

GRACE.

You'd bring but little aid, sir.

WINWIFE.

(I'll look to you i' faith, gamester.)—An unfortunate foolish tribe you are fall'n into, lady, I wonder you can endure 'em.

GRACE.

Sir, they that cannot work their fetters off, must wear 'em.

WINWIFE.

You see what care they have on you, to leave you thus.

GRACE.

Faith, the same they have of themselves, sir. I cannot greatly complain, if this were all the plea I had against 'em.

WINWIFE.

'Tis true! but will you please to withdraw with us a little, and make them think they have lost you. I hope our manners ha' been such hitherto, and our language, as will give you no cause to doubt yourself in our company.

GRACE.

Sir, I will give myself no cause; I am so secure of mine

---

273. *bought me*] from the king who could, and did, sell the guardianship of royal wards (that is, minors who were heirs to tenants holding land from the crown).

277. *disparagement*] marriage to someone of inferior rank; a guardian could enforce only a marriage "without disparagement or inequality" (Blackstone).

294. *doubt yourself*] fear.

own manners, as I suspect not yours.

QUARLOUS.
Look where John Littlewit comes.

WINWIFE.
Away, I'll not be seen, by him.

QUARLOUS.
No, you were not best, he'd tell his mother, the widow.

WINWIFE.
Heart, what do you mean?

QUARLOUS.
Cry you mercy, is the wind there? Must not the widow be nam'd? [*Exeunt* Grace, Winwife, Quarlous.]

[III.vi] [*Enter to them*] Littlewit, Win.

LITTLEWIT.
Do you hear, Win, Win?

WIN.
What say you, John?

LITTLEWIT.
While they are paying the reckoning, Win, I'll tell you a thing, Win: we shall never see any sights i' the Fair, Win, except you long still, Win; good Win, sweet Win, long to see some hobbyhorses, and some drums, and rattles, and dogs, and fine devices, Win. The bull with the five legs, Win; and the great hog: now you ha' begun with pig, you may long for anything, Win, and so for my motion, Win.

WIN.
But we sha' not eat o' the bull and the hog, John, how shall I long then?

LITTLEWIT.
O yes! Win, you may long to see, as well as to taste, Win: how did the 'pothecary's wife, Win, that long'd to see the anatomy, Win? Or the lady, Win, that desir'd to spit i' the great lawyer's mouth, after an eloquent pleading? I assure you they long'd, Win; good Win, go in, and long.
[*Exeunt* Littlewit, Win.]

[III.vi]
14. *anatomy*] skeleton.

TRASH.

I think we are rid of our new customer, brother Leatherhead, we shall hear no more of him.

They plot to be gone.

LEATHERHEAD.

All the better, let's pack up all, and be gone, before he find us.

TRASH.

Stay a little, yonder comes a company: it may be we may take some more money.

[*Enter*] Knockem, Busy.

KNOCKEM.

Sir, I will take your counsel, and cut my hair, and leave vapors: I see that tobacco, and bottle-ale, and pig, and Whit, and very Urs'la herself, is all vanity.

BUSY.

Only pig was not comprehended in my admonition, the rest were. For long hair, it is an ensign of pride, a banner, and the world is full of those banners, very full of banners. And bottle-ale is a drink of Satan's, a diet-drink of Satan's, devised to puff us up and make us swell in this latter age of vanity, as the smoke of tobacco to keep us in mist and error; but the fleshly woman (which you call Urs'la) is above all to be avoided, having the marks upon her, of the three enemies of man: the world, as being in the Fair; the devil, as being in the fire; and the flesh, as being herself.

[*Enter*] Purecraft.

PURECRAFT.

Brother Zeal-of-the-land! what shall we do? My daughter, Win-the-fight, is fall'n into her fit of longing again.

BUSY.

For more pig? There is no more, is there?

---

23. *cut my hair*] a sign of reformation to Puritans (cf. I. 27).
29. *diet-drink*] medicine.

PURECRAFT.

To see some sights, i' the Fair.

BUSY.

Sister, let her fly the impurity of the place, swiftly, lest she partake of the pitch thereof. Thou art the seat of the Beast, O Smithfield, and I will leave thee. Idolatry peepeth out on every side of thee.

KNOCKEM.

An excellent right hypocrite! now his belly is full, he falls a-railing and kicking, the jade. A very good vapor! I'll in, and joy Urs'la with telling how her pig works; two and a half he eat to his share. And he has drunk a pailful. He eats with his eyes, as well as his teeth. [*Exit.*]

LEATHERHEAD.

What do you lack, gentlemen? What is't you buy? Rattles, drums, babies—

BUSY.

Peace, with thy apocryphal wares, thou profane publican: thy bells, thy dragons, and thy Toby's dogs. Thy hobbyhorse is an idol, a very idol, a fierce and rank idol; and thou the Nebuchadnezzar, the proud Nebuchadnezzar of the Fair, that sett'st it up, for children to fall down to, and worship.

LEATHERHEAD.

Cry you mercy, sir, will you buy a fiddle to fill up your noise?

[*Re-enter* Littlewit, Win.]

LITTLEWIT.

Look, Win. Do, look o' God's name, and save your longing. Here be fine sights.

PURECRAFT.

Aye child, so you hate 'em, as our Brother Zeal does, you may look on 'em.

---

52. *apocryphal*] sham (with a reference to the Puritan rejection of the Apocrypha).

53. *Toby's dogs*] the dog in the Punch and Judy show; possibly from the *Book of Tobit*.

LEATHERHEAD.

Or what do you say to a drum, sir?

BUSY.

It is the broken belly of the Beast, and thy bellows there are his lungs, and these pipes are his throat, those feathers are of his tail, and thy rattles, the gnashing of his teeth.

TRASH.

And what's my gingerbread? I pray you.

BUSY.

The provender that pricks him up. Hence with thy basket of popery, thy nest of images: and whole legend of ginger-work.

LEATHERHEAD.

Sir, if you be not quiet the quicklier, I'll ha' you clapp'd fairly by the heels, for disturbing the Fair.

BUSY.

The sin of the Fair provokes me, I cannot be silent.

PURECRAFT.

Good brother Zeal!

LEATHERHEAD.

Sir, I'll make you silent, believe it.

LITTLEWIT.

I'd give a shilling you could, i' faith, friend.

LEATHERHEAD.

Sir, give me your shilling; I'll give you my shop, if I do not, and I'll leave it in pawn with you, i' the meantime.

LITTLEWIT.

A match i' faith, but do it quickly, then.

[*Exit* Leatherhead.]

BUSY.

Hinder me not, woman.

He speaks to the widow.

I was mov'd in spirit, to be here, this day, in this Fair, this wicked, and foul Fair (and fitter may it be called a foul,

83. be] F_3; be a *F*.

---

69. *pricks him up*] stimulates.

70. *images*] gingerbread cakes at the Fair were molded into figures of St. Bartholomew.

70. *legend*] a collection of saints' lives.

than a Fair) to protest against the abuses of it, the foul abuses of it, in regard of the afflicted saints, that are troubled, very much troubled, exceedingly troubled, with the opening of the merchandise of Babylon again, and the peeping of popery upon the stalls, here, here, in the high places. See you not Goldylocks, the purple strumpet, there, in her yellow gown, and green sleeves? The profane pipes, the tinkling timbrels? A shop of relics!

LITTLEWIT.

Pray you forbear, I am put in trust with 'em.

BUSY.

And this idolatrous grove of images, this flasket of idols! which I will pull down— *Overthrows the gingerbread.*

TRASH.

O my ware, my ware, God bless it.

BUSY.

—In my zeal, and glory to be thus exercis'd.

Leatherhead *enters with officers.*

LEATHERHEAD.

Here he is, pray you lay hold on his zeal, we cannot sell a whistle, for him, in tune. Stop his noise, first!

BUSY.

Thou canst not: 'tis a sanctified noise. I will make a loud and most strong noise, till I have daunted the profane enemy. And for this cause—

LEATHERHEAD.

Sir, here's no man afraid of you, or your cause. You shall swear it, i' the stocks, sir.

BUSY.

I will thrust myself into the stocks, upon the pikes of the land.

LEATHERHEAD.

Carry him away.

PURECRAFT.

What do you mean, wicked men?

---

89. *Goldylocks*] vaguely used for one who has golden hair.
93. *flasket*] a long shallow basket.

BUSY.

Let them alone; I fear them not.

[*Exeunt officers, with* Busy, *followed by* Purecraft.]

LITTLEWIT.

Was not this shilling well ventur'd, Win, for our liberty? Now we may go play, and see over the Fair, where we list, ourselves; my mother is gone after him, and let her e'en go, and loose us.

WIN.

Yes, John, but I know not what to do.

LITTLEWIT.

For what, Win?

WIN.

For a thing, I am asham'd to tell you, i' faith, and 'tis too far to go home.

LITTLEWIT.

I pray thee be not asham'd, Win. Come, i' faith thou shall not be asham'd; is it anything about the hobbyhorse-man? An't be, speak freely.

WIN.

Hang him, base bobchin, I scorn him; no, I have very great what sha' call 'em, John.

LITTLEWIT.

O! is that all, Win? We'll go back to Captain Jordan; to the pig-woman's, Win: he'll help us, or she with a dripping pan, or an old kettle, or something. The poor greasy soul loves you, Win, and after we'll visit the Fair all over, Win, and see my puppet-play, Win; you know it's a fine matter, Win. [*Exeunt* Littlewit, Win.]

LEATHERHEAD.

Let's away; I counsel'd you to pack up afore, Joan.

TRASH.

A pox of his Bedlam purity. He has spoil'd half my ware: but the best is, we lose nothing, if we miss our first merchant.

LEATHERHEAD.

It shall be hard for him to find, or know us, when we are translated, Joan. [*Exeunt.*]

---

131. *merchant*] customer.
133. *translated*] transformed.

[IV.i] [*Enter*] Trouble-All, Bristle, Haggis, Cokes, Justice.

TROUBLE-ALL.

My masters, I do make no doubt but you are officers.

BRISTLE.

What then, sir?

TROUBLE-ALL.

And the King's loving, and obedient subjects.

BRISTLE.

Obedient, friend? Take heed what you speak, I advise you: Oliver Bristle advises you. His loving subjects, we grant you; but not his obedient, at this time, by your leave; we know ourselves a little better than so; we are to command, sir, and such as you are to be obedient. Here's one of his obedient subjects going to the stocks, and we'll make you such another, if you talk.

TROUBLE-ALL.

You are all wise enough i' your places, I know.

BRISTLE.

If you know it, sir, why do you bring it in question?

TROUBLE-ALL.

I question nothing, pardon me. I do only hope you have warrant, for what you do, and so, quit you, and so, multiply you. *He goes away again.*

HAGGIS.

What's he? Bring him up to the stocks there. Why bring you him not up?

[Trouble-All] *comes again.*

TROUBLE-ALL.

If you have Justice Overdo's warrant, 'tis well: you are safe; that is the warrant of warrants. I'll not give this button, for any man's warrant else.

BRISTLE.

Like enough, sir; but let me tell you, an' you play away your buttons, thus, you will want 'em ere night, for any

---

5. *Oliver*] called Davy at III.i.8.

14–15. *quit . . . you*] God requite (reward) you and increase your family.

store I see about you: you might keep 'em, and save pins, I wusse. [Trouble-All] *goes away.*

JUSTICE OVERDO [*aside*].

What should he be, that doth so esteem and advance my warrant? He seems a sober and discreet person! It is a comfort to a good conscience to be follow'd with a good fame, in his sufferings. The world will have a pretty taste by this, how I can bear adversity: and it will beget a kind of reverence toward me, hereafter, even from mine enemies, when they shall see I carry my calamity nobly, and that it doth neither break me, nor bend me.

HAGGIS.

Come, sir, here's a place for you to preach in. Will you put in your leg?

They put him in the stocks.

JUSTICE OVERDO.

That I will, cheerfully.

BRISTLE.

O' my conscience, a seminary! He kisses the stocks.

COKES.

Well, my masters, I'll leave him with you; now I see him bestow'd, I'll go look for my goods, and Numps.

HAGGIS.

You may, sir, I warrant you; where's the tother bawler? fetch him too, you shall find 'em both fast enough.

[*Exit* Cokes.]

JUSTICE OVERDO [*aside*].

In the midst of this tumult, I will yet be the author of mine own rest, and not minding their fury, sit in the stocks in that calm as shall be able to trouble a triumph.

[Trouble-All] *comes again.*

TROUBLE-ALL.

Do you assure me upon your words? May I undertake for you, if I be ask'd the question; that you have this warrant?

---

23. *store*] supply.

HAGGIS.

What's this fellow, for God's sake?

TROUBLE-ALL.

Do but show me Adam Overdo, and I am satisfied. *Goes out.*

BRISTLE.

He is a fellow that is distracted, they say; one Trouble-All: he was an officer in the court of Pie-powders, here last year, and put out on his place by Justice Overdo.

JUSTICE OVERDO.

Ha!

BRISTLE.

Upon which he took an idle conceit, and's run mad upon't. So that, ever since, he will do nothing but by Justice Overdo's warrant: he will not eat a crust, nor drink a little, nor make him in his apparel ready. His wife, sir-reverence, cannot get him make his water, or shift his shirt, without his warrant.

JUSTICE OVERDO [*aside*].

If this be true, this is my greatest disaster! How am I bound to satisfy this poor man, that is of so good a nature to me, out of his wits, where there is no room left for dissembling!

[Trouble-All] *comes in.*

TROUBLE-ALL.

If you cannot show me Adam Overdo, I am in doubt of you: I am afraid you cannot answer it. *Goes again.*

HAGGIS.

Before me, neighbor Bristle, (and now I think on't better) Justice Overdo is a very parantory person.

BRISTLE.

O! are you advis'd of that? And a severe justicer, by your leave.

---

52. *idle*] foolish.

63. *answer*] make defense against.

65. *parantory*] peremptory; H.S. thinks such a spelling a suggestion of the comic "mistaking words" mentioned in the Induction, l. 44.

66. *advis'd*] aware.

JUSTICE OVERDO [*aside*].
Do I hear ill o' that side, too?

BRISTLE.
He will sit as upright o' the bench, an' you mark him, as a candle i' the socket, and give light to the whole court in every business.

HAGGIS.
But he will burn blue, and swell like a bile (God bless us) an' he be angry.

BRISTLE.
Aye, and he will be angry too, when he list, that's more: and when he is angry, be it right or wrong, he has the law on's side, ever. I mark that too.

JUSTICE OVERDO [*aside*].
I will be more tender hereafter. I see compassion may become a justice, though it be a weakness, I confess; and nearer a vice, than a virtue.

HAGGIS.
Well, take him out o' the stocks again, we'll go a sure way to work, we'll ha' the ace of hearts of our side, if we can.

They take the Justice *out.* [*Enter*] Pocher, Busy, Purecraft.

POCHER.
Come, bring him away to his fellow, there. Master Busy, we shall rule your legs, I hope, though we cannot rule your tongue.

BUSY.
No, minister of darkness, no, thou canst not rule my tongue; my tongue it is mine own, and with it I will both knock, and mock down your Bartholomew-abominations, till you be made a hissing to the neighbor parishes, round about.

HAGGIS.
Let him alone, we have devis'd better upon't.

74. he list] *E.A.H.*; his list *F*; him list *H.S.*

---

72. *blue*] pale (of candles); livid (of persons).
72. *bile*] boil.

PURECRAFT.

And shall he not into the stocks then?

BRISTLE.

No, mistress, we'll have 'em both to Justice Overdo, and let him do over 'em as is fitting. Then I, and my gossip Haggis, and my beadle Pocher are discharg'd.

PURECRAFT.

O, I thank you, blessed, honest men!

BRISTLE.

Nay, never thank us, but thank this madman that comes here, he put it in our heads.

[Trouble-All] *comes again.*

PURECRAFT.

Is he mad? Now heaven increase his madness, and bless it, and thank it: sir, your poor handmaid thanks you.

TROUBLE-ALL.

Have you a warrant? An' you have a warrant, show it.

PURECRAFT.

Yes, I have a warrant out of the word, to give thanks for removing any scorn intended to the brethren.

[*Exeunt all but* Trouble-All.]

TROUBLE-ALL.

It is Justice Overdo's warrant, that I look for: if you have not that, keep your word, I'll keep mine. Quit ye, and multiply ye.

[IV.ii]

[*Enter to him, severally*] Edgworth, Nightingale, Cokes, Costermonger.

EDGWORTH.

Come away, Nightingale, I pray thee.

TROUBLE-ALL.

Whither go you? Where's your warrant?

EDGWORTH.

Warrant, for what, sir?

---

95. *discharg'd*] relieved of responsibility.
102. *the word*] the Bible.

TROUBLE-ALL.

For what you go about; you know how fit it is; an' you have no warrant, bless you, I'll pray for you, that's all I can do. *Goes out.*

EDGWORTH.

What means he?

NIGHTINGALE.

A madman that haunts the Fair, do you not know him? It's marvel he has not more followers after his ragged heels.

EDGWORTH.

Beshrew him, he startled me: I thought he had known of our plot. Guilt's a terrible thing! Ha' you prepar'd the costermonger?

NIGHTINGALE.

Yes, and agreed for his basket of pears; he is at the corner here, ready. And your prize, he comes down, sailing, that way, all alone; without his protector: he is rid of him, it seems.

EDGWORTH.

Aye, I know; I should ha' follow'd his Protectorship for a feat I am to do upon him; but this offer'd itself so i' the way, I could not let it 'scape: here he comes, whistle; be this sport call'd "Dorring the Dottrell."

NIGHTINGALE.

Wh, wh, wh, wh, &c. Nightingale *whistles.*

COKES.

By this light, I cannot find my gingerbread-wife, nor my hobbyhorse-man, in all the Fair, now, to ha' my money again. And I do not know the way out on't, to go home for more, do you hear, friend, you that whistle? What tune is that you whistle?

NIGHTINGALE.

A new tune, I am practicing, sir.

12–13. *prepar'd the costermonger*] In *Bartholomew Faire, or Variety of Fancies* (1641) this league between cutpurses and costermongers is described.

21. *Dorring the Dottrell*] tricking the simpleton (*dor,* trick; *dottrell,* plover, a stupid bird).

COKES.

Dost thou know where I dwell, I pray thee? Nay, on with thy tune, I ha' no such haste for an answer: I'll practice with thee.

COSTERMONGER.

Buy any pears, very fine pears, pears fine.

Nightingale *sets his foot afore him, and he falls with his basket.*

COKES.

Godso! a muss, a muss, a muss, a muss.

COSTERMONGER.

Good gentleman, my ware, my ware, I am a poor man. Good sir, my ware.

NIGHTINGALE.

Let me hold your sword, sir, it troubles you.

COKES.

Do, and my cloak, an' thou wilt; and my hat, too.

Cokes *falls a-scrambling whilst they run away with his things.*

EDGWORTH.

A delicate great boy! methinks, he out-scrambles 'em all. I cannot persuade myself, but he goes to grammar school yet; and plays the truant, today.

NIGHTINGALE.

Would he had another purse to cut, 'Zekiel.

EDGWORTH.

Purse? a man might cut out his kidneys, I think; and he never feel 'em, he is so earnest at the sport.

NIGHTINGALE.

His soul is halfway out on's body, at the game.

EDGWORTH.

Away, Nightingale: that way.

[Nightingale *runs off with his sword, cloak, and hat.*]

COKES.

I think I am furnish'd for Cather'ne pears, for one under-meal: gi' me my cloak.

---

33. *muss*] scramble.
46–47. *under-meal*] afternoon; afternoon meal (cf. H.S., X, 202).

COSTERMONGER.

Good gentleman, give me my ware.

COKES.

Where's the fellow, I ga' my cloak to? My cloak? and my hat? ha! God's lid, is he gone? Thieves, thieves, help me to cry, gentlemen. *He runs out.*

EDGWORTH.

Away, costermonger, come to us to Urs'la's.

[*Exit* Costermonger.]

Talk of him to have a soul? 'Heart, if he have any more than a thing given him instead of salt, only to keep him from stinking, I'll be hang'd afore my time, presently: where should it be, trow? In his blood? He has not so much to'ard it in his whole body as will maintain a good flea; and if he take this course, he will not ha' so much land left as to rear a calf within this twelvemonth. Was there ever green plover so pull'd! That his little overseer had been here now, and been but tall enough, to see him steal pears, in exchange for his beaver hat and his cloak thus! I must go find him out, next, for his black box, and his patent (it seems) he has of his place; which I think the gentleman would have a reversion of, that spoke to me for it so earnestly. [*Exit.*]

He [Cokes] *comes again.*

COKES.

Would I might lose my doublet, and hose too, as I am an honest man, and never stir, if I think there be anything but thieving, and coz'ning, i' this whole Fair. Bartholomew-fair, quoth he; an' ever any Bartholomew had that luck in't that I have had, I'll be martyr'd for him, and in Smithfield, too.

Throws away his pears.

I ha' paid for my pears, a rot on 'em, I'll keep 'em no longer; you were choke-pears to me; I had been better

---

64. *patent*] a document conferring an office.
74. *choke-pears*] coarse pears used for perry.

ha' gone to mum-chance for you, I wusse. Methinks the Fair should not have us'd me thus, and 'twere but for my name's sake; I would not ha' us'd a dog o' the name, so. O, Numps will triumph, now!

Trouble-All comes again.

Friend, do you know who I am? Or where I lie? I do not myself, I'll be sworn. Do but carry me home, and I'll please thee, I ha' money enough there; I ha' lost myself, and my cloak and my hat; and my fine sword, and my sister, and Numps, and Mistress Grace (a gentlewoman that I should ha' married), and a cut-work handkercher she ga' me, and two purses, today. And my bargain o' hobby-horses and gingerbread, which grieves me worst of all.

TROUBLE-ALL.

By whose warrant, sir, have you done all this?

COKES.

Warrant? thou art a wise fellow, indeed; as if a man need a warrant to lose anything with.

TROUBLE-ALL.

Yes, Justice Overdo's warrant, a man may get and lose with, I'll stand to't.

COKES.

Justice Overdo? Dost thou know him? I lie there, he is my brother-in-law, he married my sister: pray thee show me the way, dost thou know the house?

TROUBLE-ALL.

Sir, show me your warrant; I know nothing without a warrant, pardon me.

COKES.

Why, I warrant thee, come along: thou shalt see I have wrought pillows there, and cambric sheets, and sweet bags, too. Pray thee guide me to the house.

TROUBLE-ALL.

Sir, I'll tell you; go you thither yourself, first, alone; tell

75. *mum-chance*] a game played with cards or dice in which silence was essential (Nares).

80. *carry*] lead.

92. *lie*] lodge.

98. *wrought*] embroidered.

your worshipful brother your mind: and but bring me three lines of his hand, or his clerk's, with "Adam Overdo" underneath; here I'll stay you; I'll obey you, and I'll guide you presently.

COKES [*aside*].

'Slid, this is an ass, I ha' found him; pox upon me, what do I talking to such a dull fool? [*to him*] Farewell, you are a very coxcomb, do you hear?

TROUBLE-ALL.

I think I am; if Justice Overdo sign to it, I am, and so we are all; he'll quit us all, multiply us all. [*Exeunt.*]

[IV.iii]

[*Enter*] Grace. Quarlous, Winwife *enter with their swords drawn.*

GRACE.

Gentlemen, this is no way that you take: you do but breed one another trouble, and offense, and give me no contentment at all. I am no she that affects to be quarrel'd for, or have my name or fortune made the question of men's swords.

QUARLOUS.

'Slood, we love you.

GRACE.

If you both love me, as you pretend, your own reason will tell you but one can enjoy me; and to that point, there leads a directer line than by my infamy, which must follow if you fight. 'Tis true, I have profess'd it to you ingenuously that, rather than to be yok'd with this bridegroom is appointed me, I would take up any husband, almost upon any trust. Though subtlety would say to me (I know) he is a fool, and has an estate, and I might govern him, and enjoy a friend beside. But these are not my aims; I must have a husband I must love, or I cannot live with him. I shall ill make one of these politic wives!

WINWIFE.

Why, if you can like either of us, lady, say which is he,

[IV.iii]

3. *affects*] likes.

17. *politic*] scheming.

and the other shall swear instantly to desist.

QUARLOUS.

Content, I accord to that willingly.

GRACE.

Sure you think me a woman of an extreme levity, gentlemen, or a strange fancy, that (meeting you by chance in such a place as this, both at one instant, and not yet of two hours' acquaintance, neither of you deserving, afore the other, of me) I should so forsake my modesty (though I might affect one more particularly) as to say, "This is he," and name him.

QUARLOUS.

Why, wherefore should you not? What should hinder you?

GRACE.

If you would not give it to my modesty, allow it yet to my wit; give me so much of woman, and cunning, as not to betray myself impertinently. How can I judge of you, so far as to a choice, without knowing you more? You are both equal and alike to me, yet; and so indifferently affected by me, as each of you might be the man, if the other were away. For you are reasonable creatures, you have understanding, and discourse. And if fate send me an understanding husband, I have no fear at all, but mine own manners shall make him a good one.

QUARLOUS.

Would I were put forth to making for you, then.

GRACE.

It may be you are, you know not what's toward you: will you consent to a motion of mine, gentlemen?

WINWIFE.

Whatever it be, we'll presume reasonableness, coming from you.

QUARLOUS.

And fitness, too.

---

36. *For*] because.
37. *discourse*] rationality.
40. *to making*] for training.
41. *toward*] in store for.
42. *motion*] suggestion.

GRACE.

I saw one of you buy a pair of tables, e'en now.

WINWIFE.

Yes, here they be, and maiden ones too, unwritten in.

GRACE.

The fitter for what they may be employed in. You shall write, either of you, here, a word, or a name, what you like best; but of two, or three syllables at most: and the next person that comes this way (because destiny has a high hand in business of this nature) I'll demand, which of the two words he or she doth approve; and according to that sentence, fix my resolution, and affection, without change.

QUARLOUS.

Agreed, my word is conceived already.

WINWIFE.

And mine shall not be long creating after.

GRACE.

But you shall promise, gentlemen, not to be curious to know, which of you it is, is taken; but give me leave to conceal that till you have brought me, either home, or where I may safely tender myself.

WINWIFE.

Why, that's but equal.

QUARLOUS.

We are pleas'd.

GRACE.

Because I will bind both your endeavors to work together, friendly, and jointly, each to the other's fortune, and have myself fitted with some means to make him that is forsaken a part of amends.

QUARLOUS.

These conditions are very courteous. Well, my word is out of the *Arcadia,* then: "Argalus."

59. is, is taken] *H.S.*; is, taken *F.*

---

46. *tables*] writing tablets.
61. *tender*] take care of.
62. *equal*] fair.
69. *Argalus*] lover of Parthenia in Sidney's *Arcadia* (1590).

WINWIFE.

And mine out of the play, "Palemon."

Trouble-All *comes again.*

TROUBLE-ALL.

Have you any warrant for this, gentlemen?

QUARLOUS. WINWIFE.

Ha!

TROUBLE-ALL.

There must be a warrant had, believe it.

WINWIFE.

For what?

TROUBLE-ALL.

For whatsoever it is, anything indeed, no matter what.

QUARLOUS.

'Slight, here's a fine ragged prophet, dropp'd down i' the nick!

TROUBLE-ALL.

Heaven quit you, gentlemen.

QUARLOUS.

Nay, stay a little: good lady, put him to the question.

GRACE.

You are content, then?

WINWIFE. QUARLOUS.

Yes, yes.

GRACE.

Sir, here are two names written—

TROUBLE-ALL.

Is Justice Overdo, one?

GRACE.

How, sir? I pray you read 'em to yourself; it is for a wager between these gentlemen; and with a stroke or any difference, mark which you approve best.

TROUBLE-ALL.

They may be both worshipful names for ought I know,

83. Justice] F_3; *Iudice F.*

70. *play*] probably the *Two Noble Kinsmen* (1613).
86. *difference*] distinguishing mark.

mistress, but Adam Overdo had been worth three of 'em, I assure you, in this place; that's in plain English.

GRACE.

This man amazes me! I pray you, like one of 'em, sir.

TROUBLE-ALL.

I do like him there, that has the best warrant. Mistress, to save your longing (and multiply him), it may be this. [*Marks the book.*] But I am aye still for Justice Overdo, that's my conscience. And quit you. [*Exit.*]

WINWIFE.

Is't done, lady?

GRACE.

Aye, and strangely, as ever I saw! What fellow is this, trow?

QUARLOUS.

No matter what, a fortuneteller we ha' made him. Which is't, which is't?

GRACE.

Nay, did you not promise, not to inquire?

[*Enter*] Edgworth.

QUARLOUS.

'Slid, I forgot that, pray you pardon me. Look, here's our Mercury come: the license arrives i' the finest time, too! 'Tis but scraping out Cokes his name, and 'tis done.

WINWIFE.

How now, lime-twig? Hast thou touch'd?

EDGWORTH.

Not yet, sir; except you would go with me, and see't, it's not worth speaking on. The act is nothing, without a witness. Yonder he is, your man with the box fall'n into the finest company, and so transported with vapors; they ha' got in a northern clothier, and one Puppy, a western man, that's come to wrestle before my Lord Mayor anon, and Captain Whit, and one Val Cutting, that helps Cap-

---

104. *lime-twigs*] twigs were covered with birdlime to catch birds; here, by metonymy, a thief.

110. *wrestle . . . Mayor*] an important event on St. Bartholomew's Day.

tain Jordan to roar, a circling boy: with whom your Numps is so taken, that you may strip him of his clothes, if you will. I'll undertake to geld him for you; if you had but a surgeon, ready, to sear him. And Mistress Justice, there, is the goodest woman! She does so love 'em all over, in terms of Justice, and the style of authority, with her hood upright—that I beesech you come away, gentlemen, and see't.

QUARLOUS.
'Slight, I would not lose it for the Fair; what'll you do, Ned?

WINWIFE.
Why, stay here about for you; Mistress Wellborn must not be seen.

QUARLOUS.
Do so, and find out a priest i' the meantime; I'll bring the license. Lead, which way is't?

EDGWORTH.
Here, sir, you are o' the backside o' the booth already, you may hear the noise. [*Exeunt.*]

[IV.iv]

[*Enter*] Knockem, Nordern, Puppy, Cutting, Whit, Wasp, Mistress Overdo.

KNOCKEM.
Whit, bid Val Cutting continue the vapors for a lift, Whit, for a lift.

NORDERN.
I'll ne mare, I'll ne mare, the eale's too meeghty.

KNOCKEM.
How now! my Galloway Nag, the staggers? Ha! Whit, gi' him a slit i' the forehead. Cheer up, man; a needle and thread to stitch his ears. I'd cure him now an' I had it,

---

112. *circling boy*] a roarer and a thief's decoy? (cf. IV.iv.123–125).

[IV.iv]

1. *lift*] theft; trick.

4. *Galloway Nag*] a small hardy breed of Scotch horses.

5–6. *slit . . . ears*] two cures for the staggers, a cerebral disease in horses: slitting open the forehead; or stopping up the ears with medi-

with a little butter, and garlic, long-pepper, and grains. Where's my horn? I'll gi' him a mash, presently, shall take away this dizziness.

PUPPY.

Why, where are you, zurs? Do you vlinch, and leave us i' the zuds, now?

NORDERN.

I'll ne mare, I is e'en as vull as a paiper's bag, by my troth, aye.

PUPPY.

Do my northern cloth zhrink i' the wetting, ha?

KNOCKEM.

Why, well said, old flea-bitten, thou'lt never tire, I see.

They fall to their vapors, again.

CUTTING.

No, sir, but he may tire, if it please him.

WHIT.

Who told dee sho? that he vuld never teer, man?

CUTTING.

No matter who told him so, so long as he knows.

KNOCKEM.

Nay, I know nothing, sir, pardon me there.

[*Enter*] Edgworth, Quarlous.

EDGWORTH.

They are at it still, sir, this they call vapors.

WHIT.

He shall not pardon dee, captain, dou shalt not be pardon'd. Pre'dee shweetheart, do not pardon him.

CUTTING.

'Slight, I'll pardon him, an' I list, whosoever says nay to't.

QUARLOUS.

Where's Numps? I miss him.

---

cine, then stitching the tips together to keep the horse from shaking the medicine out (Markham, 64).

8. *horn*] used for dosing horses.

10–11. *i' the zuds*] in difficulties.

15. *flea-bitten*] proverbial: "A flea-bitten horse never tires."

WASP.

Why, I say nay to't.

QUARLOUS.

O there he is!

KNOCKEM.

To what do you say nay, sir?

Here they continue their game of vapors, which is nonsense: every man to oppose the last man that spoke, whether it concern'd him, or no.

WASP.

To anything, whatsoever it is, so long as I do not like it.

WHIT.

Pardon me, little man, dou musht like it a little.

CUTTING.

No, he must not like it at all, sir; there you are i' the wrong.

WHIT.

I tink I be, he musht not like it, indeed.

CUTTING.

Nay, then he both must, and will like it, sir, for all you.

KNOCKEM.

If he have reason, he may like it, sir.

WHIT.

By no meansh, captain, upon reason, he may like nothing upon reason.

WASP.

I have no reason, nor I will hear of no reason, nor I will look for no reason, and he is an ass that either knows any, or looks for't from me.

CUTTING.

Yes, in some sense you may have reason, sir.

WASP.

Aye, in some sense, I care not if I grant you.

WHIT.

Pardon me, thou ougsht to grant him nothing, in no shensh, if dou do love dyshelf, angry man.

WASP.

Why then, I do grant him nothing; and I have no sense.

CUTTING.

'Tis true, thou hast no sense indeed.

WASP.

'Slid, but I have sense, now I think on't better, and I will grant him anything, do you see?

KNOCKEM.

He is i' the right, and does utter a sufficient vapor.

CUTTING.

Nay, it is no sufficient vapor, neither, I deny that.

KNOCKEM.

Then it is a sweet vapor.

CUTTING.

It may be a sweet vapor.

WASP.

Nay, it is no sweet vapor, neither, sir; it stinks, and I'll stand to't.

WHIT.

Yes, I tink it dosh shtink, Captain. All vapor dosh shtink.

WASP.

Nay, then it does not stink, sir, and it shall not stink.

CUTTING.

By your leave, it may, sir.

WASP.

Aye, by my leave, it may stink; I know that.

WHIT.

Pardon me, thou knowesht nothing; it cannot by thy leave, angry man.

WASP.

How can it not?

KNOCKEM.

Nay, never question him, for he is i' the right.

WHIT.

Yesh, I am i' de right, I confesh it; so ish de little man too.

WASP.

I'll have nothing confess'd that concerns me. I am not i' the right, nor never was i' the right, nor never will be i' the right, while I am in my right mind.

CUTTING.

Mind? Why, here's no man minds you, sir, nor anything else.

They drink again.

PUPPY.

Vriend, will you mind this that we do?

QUARLOUS.

Call you this vapors? This is such belching of quarrel, as I never heard. Will you mind your business, sir?

EDGWORTH.

You shall see, sir.

NORDERN.

I'll ne mair, my waimb warks too mickle with this auready.

EDGWORTH.

Will you take that, Master Wasp, that nobody should mind you?

WASP.

Why? What ha' you to do? Is't any matter to you?

EDGWORTH.

No, but methinks you should not be unminded, though.

WASP.

Nor I wu' not be, now I think on't; do you hear, new acquaintance, does no man mind me, say you?

CUTTING.

Yes, sir, every man here minds you, but how?

WASP.

Nay, I care as little how, as you do; that was not my question.

WHIT.

No, noting was ty question; tou art a learned man, and I am a valiant man, i' faith la, tou shalt speak for me, and I vill fight for tee.

KNOCKEM.

Fight for him, Whit? A gross vapor; he can fight for himself.

WASP.

It may be I can, but it may be, I wu' not, how then?

CUTTING.

Why, then you may choose.

WASP.

Why, and I'll choose whether I'll choose or no.

KNOCKEM.

I think you may, and 'tis true; and I allow it for a resolute vapor.

WASP.

Nay, then, I do think you do not think, and it is no resolute vapor.

CUTTING.

Yes, in some sort he may allow you.

KNOCKEM.

In no sort, sir, pardon me, I can allow him nothing. You mistake the vapor.

WASP.

He mistakes nothing, sir, in no sort.

WHIT.

Yes, I pre dee now, let him mistake.

WASP.

A turd i' your teeth, never pre dee me, for I will have nothing mistaken.

KNOCKEM.

Turd, ha, turd? A noisome vapor; strike, Whit.

They fall by the ears.

[Edgworth *steals the license out of the box, and exit.*]

MRS. OVERDO.

Why, gentlemen, why gentlemen, I charge you upon my authority, conserve the peace. In the king's name, and my husband's, put up your weapons; I shall be driven to commit you myself, else.

QUARLOUS.

Ha, ha, ha.

WASP.

Why do you laugh, sir?

---

108. *commit*] send to prison.

QUARLOUS.

Sir, you'll allow me my Christian liberty, I may laugh, I hope.

CUTTING.

In some sort you may, and in some sort you may not, sir.

KNOCKEM.

Nay, in some sort, sir, he may neither laugh nor hope, in this company.

WASP.

Yes, then he may both laugh and hope in any sort, an't please him.

QUARLOUS.

Faith, and I will then, for it doth please me exceedingly.

WASP.

No exceeding neither, sir.

KNOCKEM.

No, that vapor is too lofty.

QUARLOUS.

Gentlemen, I do not play well at your game of vapors, I am not very good at it, but—

CUTTING.

Do you hear, sir? I would speak with you in circle!

He draws a circle on the ground.

QUARLOUS.

In circle, sir? What would you with me in circle?

CUTTING.

Can you lend me a piece, a jacobus, in circle?

QUARLOUS.

'Slid, your circle will prove more costly than your vapors, then. Sir, no, I lend you none.

CUTTING.

Your beard's not well turn'd up, sir.

QUARLOUS.

How, rascal? Are you playing with my beard? I'll break circle with you.

113, 114. *sort*] kind; group.
123. *in circle*] a challenge: to enter the circle is to offer to fight?
125. *jacobus*] the gold sovereign of James I.

They draw all, and fight.

PUPPY. NORDERN.

Gentlemen, gentlemen!

KNOCKEM.

Gather up, Whit, gather up, Whit, good vapors. [*Exit.*]

MRS. OVERDO.

What mean you? are you rebels? gentlemen! Shall I send out a sergeant-at-arms, or a writ o' rebellion, against you? I'll commit you, upon my womanhood, for a riot, upon my justice-hood, if you persist. [*Exeunt* Quarlous, Cutting.]

WASP.

Upon your justice-hood? Marry shit o' your hood; you'll commit? Spoke like a true Justice of Peace's wife, indeed, and a fine female lawyer! Turd i' your teeth for a fee, now.

MRS. OVERDO.

Why, Numps, in Master Overdo's name, I charge you.

WASP.

Good Mistress Underdo, hold your tongue.

MRS. OVERDO.

Alas! poor Numps.

WASP.

Alas! And why alas from you, I beseech you? Or why poor Numps, Goody Rich? Am I come to be pitied by your tuft taffeta now? Why mistress, I knew Adam, the clerk, your husband, when he was Adam scrivener, and writ for twopence a sheet, as high as he bears his head now, or you your hood, dame. What are you, sir?

The watch comes in.

BRISTLE.

We be men, and no infidels; what is the matter, here, and the noises? Can you tell?

---

138. *commit*] quibble on "fornicate"? (cf. 1. 142).

145. *Rich*] to the Rich family had been given, at the dissolution of the monasteries, the site and house of St. Bartholomew and hence the rights and tolls of the part of the Fair held within its premises, especially the Cloth Fair (Morley, pp. 117–118).

146. *tuft taffeta*] a richer taffeta woven with raised stripes or spots.

WASP.
Heart, what ha' you to do? Cannot a man quarrel in quietness, but he must be put out on't by you? What are you?

BRISTLE.
Why, we be His Majesty's Watch, sir.

WASP.
Watch? 'Sblood, you are a sweet watch, indeed. A body would think, and you watch'd well o' nights, you should be contented to sleep at this time o' day. Get you to your fleas, and your flock-beds, you rogues, your kennels, and lie down close.

BRISTLE.
Down? Yes, we will down, I warrant you; down with him in His Majesty's name, down, down with him, and carry him away, to the pigeon-holes.

MRS. OVERDO.
I thank you honest friends, in the behalf o' the Crown, and the peace, and in Master Overdo's name, for suppressing enormities.

WHIT.
Stay, Bristle, here ish a noder brash o' drunkards, but very quiet, special drunkards, will pay dee five shillings very well. Take 'em to dee, in de graish o' God: one of 'em does change cloth for ale in the Fair here, te oder ish a strong man, a mighty man, my Lord Mayor's man, and a wrastler. He has wrashled so long with the bottle, here, that the man with the beard hash almosht streek up hish heelsh.

BRISTLE.
'Slid the Clerk o' the Market has been to cry him all the Fair over, here, for my Lord's service.

WHIT.
Tere he ish, pre dee taik him hensh, and make ty best on him. [*Exit watch with* Wasp, Nordern, Puppy.]

---

159. *flock-beds*] beds made of coarse tufts of wool or cotton.
163. *pigeon-holes*] stocks.
173. *man . . . beard*] a drinking jug made to look like a bearded face.
175. *Clerk . . . Market*] official manager of the Fair.

How now, woman o' shilk, vat ailsh ty shweet faish? Art tou melancholy?

MRS. OVERDO.

A little distemper'd with these enormities; shall I entreat a courtesy of you, Captain?

WHIT.

Entreat a hundred, velvet voman, I vill do it, shpeak out.

MRS. OVERDO.

I cannot with modesty speak it out, but—

WHIT.

I vill do it, and more, and more, for dee. What, Urs'la, and't be bitch, and't be bawd, and't be!

[*Enter*] Ursula.

URSULA.

How now, rascal? What roar you for? Old pimp.

WHIT.

Here, put up de cloaks, Ursh; de purchase; pre dee now, shweet Ursh, help dis good brave voman to a jordan, and't be.

URSULA.

'Slid, call your Captain Jordan to her, can you not?

WHIT.

Nay, pre dee leave dy consheits, and bring the velvet woman to de—

URSULA.

I bring her! Hang her: heart, must I find a common pot for every punk i' your purlieus?

WHIT.

O good voordsh, Ursh, it ish a guest o' velvet, i' fait la.

URSULA.

Let her sell her hood, and buy a sponge, with a pox to her, my vessel is employed, sir. I have but one, and 'tis the bottom of an old bottle. An honest proctor and his wife are at it, within; if she'll stay her time, so.

198. vessel is] F_3; vessell, *F*.

---

186. *and't be*] if you are.
195. *purlieus*] suburbs, then notorious for vice.

WHIT.

As soon ash tou cansht, shweet Ursh. Of a valiant man I tink I am the patientsh man i' the world, or in all Smithfield.

[*Re-enter* Knockem.]

KNOCKEM.

How now, Whit? Close vapors, stealing your leaps? Covering in corners, ha?

WHIT.

No, fait, captain, dough tou beesht a vishe man, dy vit is a mile hence, now. I vas procuring a shmall courtesy, for a woman of fashion here.

MRS. OVERDO.

Yes, captain, though I am Justice of Peace's wife, I do love men of war, and the sons of the sword, when they come before my husband.

KNOCKEM.

Say'st thou so, filly? Thou shalt have a leap presently; I'll horse thee myself, else.

URSULA.

Come, will you bring her in now? And let her take her turn?

WHIT.

Gramercy, good Ursh, I tank dee.

MRS. OVERDO.

Master Overdo shall thank her. [*Exit.*]

[IV.v] [*Enter to them*] Littlewit, Win.

LITTLEWIT.

Good Gammer Urs; Win and I are exceedingly beholden to you, and to Captain Jordan, and Captain Whit. Win, I'll be bold to leave you i' this good company, Win: for half an hour, or so, Win, while I go, and see how my matter goes forward, and if the puppets be perfect: and then I'll come and fetch you, Win.

214. take] *1716*; talke *F*.

205. *Covering*] copulating (of stallions).

WIN.

Will you leave me alone with two men, John?

LITTLEWIT.

Aye, they are honest gentlemen, Win, Captain Jordan, and Captain Whit, they'll use you very civilly, Win; God b' w' you, Win. [*Exit.*]

URSULA.

What's her husband gone?

KNOCKEM.

On his false gallop, Urs, away.

URSULA.

An' you be right Bartholomew-birds, now show yourselves so: we are undone for want of fowl i' the Fair, here. Here will be 'Zekiel Edgworth, and three or four gallants with him at night, and I ha' neither plover nor quail for 'em: persuade this between you two, to become a bird o' the game, while I work the velvet woman within (as you call her). [*Exit.*]

KNOCKEM.

I conceive thee, Urs! go thy ways. Dost thou hear, Whit? is't not pity my delicate dark chestnut here—with the fine lean head, large forehead, round eyes, even mouth, sharp ears, long neck, thin crest, close withers, plain back, deep sides, short fillets, and full flanks; with a round belly, a plump buttock, large thighs, knit knees, straight legs, short pasterns, smooth hoofs, and short heels—should lead a dull honest woman's life, that might live the life of a lady?

WHIT.

Yes, by my fait and trot it is, captain: de honesht woman's life is a scurvy dull life, indeed, la.

WIN.

How, sir? Is an honest woman's life a scurvy life?

WHIT.

Yes, fait, shweetheart, believe him, de leef of a bondwoman! But if dou vilt harken to me, I vill make tee a

---

11. *What's*] for what purpose is.
12. *false gallop*] canter.
16. *plover, quail*] loose women.

free-woman, and a lady: dou shalt live like a lady, as te captain saish.

KNOCKEM.

Aye, and be honest too, sometimes: have her wires, and her tires, her green gowns, and velvet petticoats.

WHIT.

Aye, and ride to Ware and Rumford i' dy coash, shee de players, be in love vit 'em; sup vit gallantsh, be drunk, and cost dee noting.

KNOCKEM.

Brave vapors!

WHIT.

And lie by twenty on 'em if dou pleash, shweetheart.

WIN.

What, and be honest still? That were fine sport.

WHIT.

Tish common, shweetheart, tou may'st do it, by my hand; it shall be justified to ty husband's faish, now: tou shalt be as honesht as the skin between his hornsh, la!

KNOCKEM.

Yes, and wear a dressing, top, and topgallant, to compare with e'er a husband on 'em all, for a foretop: it is the vapor of spirit in the wife, to cuckold, nowadays; as it is the vapor of fashion, in the husband, not to suspect. Your prying cat-eyed-citizen is an abominable vapor.

WIN.

Lord, what a fool have I been!

WHIT.

Mend then, and do everyting like a lady, hereafter; never know ty husband, from another man.

KNOCKEM.

Nor any one man from another, but i' the dark.

WHIT.

Aye, and then it ish no dishgrash to know any man.

---

36. *wires*] a frame of wire to support the hair or the ruff.
37. *tires*] head dresses.
37. *green gowns*] with a quibble on grass stain.
38. *Ware and Rumford*] favorite places for assignations.
47. *top, and topgallant*] in full sail.

[*Re-enter Ursula.*]

URSULA.

Help, help here.

KNOCKEM.

How now? What vapor's there?

URSULA.

O, you are a sweet ranger! and look well to your walks. Yonder is your punk of Turnbull, Ramping Alice, has fall'n upon the poor gentlewoman within, and pull'd her hood over her ears, and her hair through it.

Alice *enters, beating the Justice's wife.*

MRS. OVERDO.

Help, help, i' the King's name.

ALICE.

A mischief on you, they are such as you are, that undo us, and take our trade from us, with your tuft taffeta haunches.

KNOCKEM.

How now, Alice!

ALICE.

The poor common whores can ha' no traffic, for the privy rich ones; your caps and hoods of velvet call away our customers, and lick the fat from us.

URSULA.

Peace, you foul ramping jade, you—

ALICE.

Od's foot, you bawd in grease, are you talking?

KNOCKEM.

Why, Alice, I say.

ALICE.

Thou sow of Smithfield, thou.

URSULA.

Thou tripe of Turnbull.

KNOCKEM.

Cat-a-mountain-vapors! ha!

---

72. *in grease*] fat; in prime condition.
76. *Cat-a-mountain*] panther.

URSULA.

You know where you were taw'd lately, both lash'd and slash'd you were in Bridewell.

ALICE.

Aye, by the same token, you rid that week, and broke out the bottom o' the cart, night-tub.

KNOCKEM.

Why, lion face! ha! do you know who I am? Shall I tear ruff, slit waistcoat, make rags of petticoat! Ha! go to, vanish, for fear of vapors. Whit, a kick, Whit, in the parting vapor. [*They kick out Alice.*] Come, brave woman, take a good heart, thou shalt be a lady, too.

WHIT.

Yes, fait, dey shall all both be ladies, and write Madam. I vill do't myself for dem. Do, is the vord, and D is the middle letter of Madam, DD, put 'em together and make deeds, without which all words are alike, la.

KNOCKEM.

'Tis true, Urs'la, take 'em in, open thy wardrope, and fit 'em to their calling. Green gowns, crimson petticoats, green women! my Lord Mayor's green women! guests o' the game, true bred. I'll provide you a coach, to take the air in.

WIN.

But do you think you can get one?

KNOCKEM.

O, they are as common as wheelbarrows where there are great dunghills. Every pettifogger's wife has 'em, for first he buys a coach, that he may marry, and then he marries that he may be made cuckold in't: for if their wives ride not to their cuckolding, they do 'em no credit. Hide, and be hidden; ride, and be ridden, says the vapor of experience. [*Exeunt* Ursula, Win, Mistress Overdo.]

---

77. *taw'd*] softened by beating.

78. *Bridewell*] prison for bawds, rogues, and whores.

79. *rid*] whores rode to prison in a cart. 80. *night-tub*] tub for filth.

82. *waistcoat*] a short garment worn about the upper part of the body; when worn without an outer gown, apparently the mark of prostitutes, sometimes called "waistcoateers" (*OED*).

90. *wardrope*] wardrobe.

[IV.vi] [*Enter*] Trouble-All.

TROUBLE-ALL.
By what warrant does it say so?

KNOCKEM.
Ha! mad child o' the Pie-powders, art thou there? Fill us a fresh can, Urs, we may drink together.

TROUBLE-ALL.
I may not drink without a warrant, captain.

KNOCKEM.
'Slood, thou'll not stale without a warrant, shortly. Whit, give me pen, ink and paper. I'll draw him a warrant presently.

TROUBLE-ALL.
It must be Justice Overdo's!

KNOCKEM.
I know, man. Fetch the drink, Whit.

WHIT.
I pre dee now, be very brief, captain; for de new ladies stay for dee.

KNOCKEM.
O, as brief as can be, here 'tis already. Adam Overdo.

TROUBLE-ALL.
Why, now, I'll pledge you, captain.

KNOCKEM.
Drink it off. I'll come to thee, anon, again. [*Exeunt.*]

[*Enter*] Quarlous, Edgworth.

QUARLOUS.
Well, sir. You are now discharg'd: beware of being spied, hereafter. Quarlous *to the cutpurse.*

EDGWORTH.
Sir, will it please you, enter in here, at Urs'la's; and take part of a silken gown, a velvet petticoat, or a wrought smock; I am promis'd such: and I can spare any gentle-

---

5. *stale*] urinate. 7. *presently*] at once.
17–18. *take part of*] partake of.

man a moiety.

QUARLOUS.

Keep it for your companions in beastliness, I am none of 'em, sir. If I had not already forgiven you a greater trespass, or thought you yet worth my beating, I would instruct your manners, to whom you made your offers. But go your ways, talk not to me, the hangman is only fit to discourse with you; the hand of beadle is too merciful a punishment for your trade of life. [*Exit* Edgworth.] I am sorry I employ'd this fellow; for he thinks me such: *Facinus quos inquinat, aequat.* But, it was for sport. And would I make it serious, the getting of this license is nothing to me, without other circumstances concur. I do think how impertinently I labor, if the word be not mine that the ragged fellow mark'd: and what advantage I have given Ned Winwife in this time now, of working her, though it be mine. He'll go near to form to her what a debauch'd rascal I am, and fright her out of all good conceit of me: I should do so by him, I am sure, if I had the opportunity. But my hope is in her temper, yet; and it must needs be next to despair, that is grounded on any part of a woman's discretion. I would give, by my troth, now, all I could spare (to my clothes, and my sword) to meet my tatter'd soothsayer again, who was my judge i' the question, to know certainly whose word he has damn'd or sav'd. For, till then, I live but under a reprieve. I must seek him. Who be these?

Enter Wasp *with the officers.*

WASP.

Sir, you are a Welsh cuckold, and a prating runt, and no constable.

---

20. *moiety*] a share.
29. *Facinus . . . aequat*] Lucan *Pharsalia* v. 290: "Crime levels those whom it pollutes" (J. D. Duff).
32. *impertinently*] to no purpose.
35. *form*] formulate.
46. *runt*] ignorant, uncouth person.

BRISTLE.

You say very well. Come put in his leg in the middle roundel, and let him hole there.

WASP.

You stink of leeks, metheglin, and cheese. You rogue.

BRISTLE.

Why, what is that to you, if you sit sweetly in the stocks in the meantime? If you have a mind to stink too, your breeches sit close enough to your bum. Sit you merry, sir.

QUARLOUS.

How now, Numps?

WASP.

It is no matter, how; pray you look off.

QUARLOUS.

Nay, I'll not offend you, Numps. I thought you had sat there to be seen.

WASP.

And to be sold, did you not? Pray you mind your business, an' you have any.

QUARLOUS.

Cry you mercy, Numps. Does you leg lie high enough?

BRISTLE.

How now, neighbor Haggis, what says Justice Overdo's worship, to the other offenders?

HAGGIS.

Why, he says just nothing, what should he say? Or where should he say? He is not to be found, man. He ha' not been seen i' the Fair, here, all this livelong day, never since seven o'clock i' the morning. His clerks know not what to think on't. There is no court of Pie-powders yet. Here they be return'd.

[*Enter others of the watch with* Justice *and* Busy.]

BRISTLE.

What shall be done with 'em, then, in your discretion?

HAGGIS.

I think we were best put 'em in the stocks, in discretion

---

50. *metheglin*] Welsh mead.
69, 70, 71. *discretion*] judgment; prudence; separation.

(there they will be safe in discretion) for the valor of an hour, or such a thing, till his worship come.

BRISTLE.

It is but a hole matter if we do, neighbor Haggis; come, sir, here is company for you; heave up the stocks.

WASP [*aside*].

I shall put a trick upon your Welsh diligence, perhaps.

As they open the stocks, Wasp *puts his shoe on his hand, and slips it in for his leg.*

BRISTLE.

Put in your leg, sir.

QUARLOUS.

What, Rabbi Busy! Is he come?

They bring Busy, *and put him in.*

BUSY.

I do obey thee; the lion may roar, but he cannot bite. I am glad to be thus separated from the heathen of the land, and put apart in the stocks, for the holy cause.

WASP.

What are you, sir?

BUSY.

One that rejoiceth in his affliction, and sitteth here to prophesy the destruction of Fairs and May-games, Wakes, and Whitsun-ales, and doth sigh and groan for the reformation of these abuses.

[*They put* Justice *in the stocks.*]

WASP.

And do you sigh and groan too, or rejoice in your affliction?

JUSTICE OVERDO.

I do not feel it, I do not think of it, it is a thing without me. Adam, thou art above these batt'ries, these contume-

71. *valor*] amount.

88–89. *a thing without me*] "the lofty language of Stoicism. He begins with the distinctions of Epictetus" (G.): that is, things under our control and things not under our control.

lies. *In te manca ruit fortuna,* as thy friend Horace says; thou art one, *Quem neque pauperies, neque mors, neque vincula terrent.* And therefore, as another friend of thine says (I think it be thy friend Persius), *Non te quaesiveris extra.*

QUARLOUS.

What's here! A stoic i' the stocks? The fool is turn'd philosopher.

BUSY.

Friend, I will leave to communicate my spirit with you, if I hear any more of those superstitious relics, those lists of Latin, the very rags of Rome, and patches of Popery.

WASP.

Nay, an' you begin to quarrel, gentlemen, I'll leave you. I ha' paid for quarreling too lately: look you, a device, but shifting in a hand for a foot. God b' w' you.

He gets out.

BUSY.

Wilt thou then leave thy brethren in tribulation?

WASP.

For this once, sir. [*Exit.*]

BUSY.

Thou art a halting neutral—stay him there, stop him—that will not endure the heat of persecution.

BRISTLE.

How now, what's the matter?

BUSY.

He is fled, he is fled, and dares not sit it out.

BRISTLE.

What, has he made an escape? Which way? Follow, neighbor Haggis. [*Exit* Haggis.]

90–92. *In . . . terrent*] adapting Horace *Sat.* II. vii. 83–88: "Who, then, is free? Only the wise man who has full command of himself; whom poverty or death or chains cannot terrify. . . . In her attacks on you fortune can do no harm except to herself."

93–94. *Non . . . extra*] Persius *Sat.* I. 7: "Look to no one outside yourself" (G. G. Ramsay).

98. *lists*] strips (of cloth).

[*Enter*] Purecraft.

PURECRAFT.

O me! In the stocks! Have the wicked prevail'd?

BUSY.

Peace, religious sister, it is my calling, comfort yourself, an extraordinary calling, and done for my better standing, my surer standing, hereafter.

The madman enters.

TROUBLE-ALL.

By whose warrant, by whose warrant, this?

QUARLOUS.

O, here's my man dropp'd in, I look'd for.

JUSTICE OVERDO.

Ha!

PURECRAFT.

O good sir, they have set the faithful, here, to be won-der'd at; and provided holes, for the holy of the land.

TROUBLE-ALL.

Had they warrant for it? Show'd they Justice Overdo's hand? If they had no warrant, they shall answer it.

[*Re-enter* Haggis.]

BRISTLE.

Sure you did not lock the stocks sufficiently, neighbor Toby!

HAGGIS.

No! See if you can lock 'em better.

BRISTLE.

They are very sufficiently lock'd, and truly, yet something is in the matter.

TROUBLE-ALL.

True, your warrant is the matter that is in question; by what warrant?

BRISTLE.

Madman, hold your peace; I will put you in his room else, in the very same hole, do you see?

QUARLOUS.

How! Is he a madman?

TROUBLE-ALL.

Show me Justice Overdo's warrant, I obey you.

HAGGIS.

You are a mad fool, hold your tongue.

[*Exeunt* Haggis, Bristle.]

TROUBLE-ALL.

In Justice Overdo's name, I drink to you, and here's my warrant. *Shows his can.*

JUSTICE OVERDO [*aside*].

Alas, poor wretch! How it earns my heart for him!

QUARLOUS [*aside*]

If he be mad, it is in vain to question him. I'll try, though. [*to him*] Friend, there was a gentlewoman show'd you two names, some hour since, Argalus and Palemon, to mark in a book; which of 'em was it you mark'd?

TROUBLE-ALL.

I mark no name, but Adam Overdo; that is the name of names; he only is the sufficient magistrate; and that name I reverence; show it me.

QUARLOUS [*aside*].

This fellow's mad indeed: I am further off, now, than afore.

JUSTICE OVERDO [*aside*].

I shall not breathe in peace, till I have made him some amends.

QUARLOUS [*aside*].

Well, I will make another use of him, is come in my head: I have a nest of beards in my trunk, one something like his.

The watchmen come back again.

BRISTLE.

This mad fool has made me that I know not whether I have lock'd the stocks or no; I think I lock'd 'em.

151–152. I have] F_3; I I haue *F*.

---

136. *earns*] grieves.
149. *nest*] collection.
149. *trunk*] trunk-hose, stuffed breeches reaching to the knees.

TROUBLE-ALL.
Take Adam Overdo in your mind, and fear nothing.

BRISTLE.
'Slid, madness itself, hold thy peace, and take that.

TROUBLE-ALL.
Strikest thou without a warrant? Take thou that.

The madman fights with 'em, and they leave open the stocks.

BUSY.
We are delivered by miracle; fellow in fetters, let us not refuse the means; this madness was of the spirit: the malice of the enemy hath mock'd itself.

[*Exeunt* Busy *and* Justice.]

PURECRAFT.
Mad, do they call him! The world is mad in error, but he is mad in truth: I love him o' the sudden (the cunning man said all true) and shall love him more, and more. How well it becomes a man to be mad in truth! O, that I might be his yoke-fellow, and be mad with him, what a many should we draw to madness in truth, with us. [*Exit.*]

The watch, missing them, are affrighted.

BRISTLE.
How now! All 'scap'd? Where's the woman? It is witchcraft! Her velvet hat is a witch, o' my conscience, or my key, t' one! The madman was a devil, and I am an ass; so bless me, my place, and mine office. [*Exeunt.*]

[V.i] [*Enter*] Leatherhead, Filcher, Sharkwell.

LEATHERHEAD.
Well, Luck and Saint Bartholomew! Out with the sign of

[V.i]
0.1. Leatherhead] *In Act V of F. Leatherhead is called* "Lanthorne" *or* "Lanterne" *in stage directions (except at* V.iii.51.1), *and "Lan." in the speech-headings; in this edition* "LEATHERHEAD" *is always used.*

---

167. *t' one*] the one or the other.
[V.i]
1. *sign*] the "banner" of I. 5.

our invention, in the name of Wit, and do you beat the drum, the while; all the foul i' the Fair, I mean all the dirt in Smithfield (that's one of Master Littlewit's carwhitchets now), will be thrown at our banner today, if the matter does not please the people. O the motions, that I Lantern Leatherhead have given light to, i' my time, since my Master Pod died! *Jerusalem* was a stately thing; and so was *Ninive,* and *The City of Norwich,* and *Sodom and Gomorrah*; with the rising o' the prentices, and pulling down the bawdy houses there, upon Shrove Tuesday; but *The Gunpowder Plot,* there was a get-penny! I have presented that to an eighteen, or twentypence audience, nine times in an afternoon. Your home-born projects prove ever the best, they are so easy, and familiar; they put too much learning i' their things now o' days: and that I fear will be the spoil o' this. Littlewit? I say, Micklewit! if not too mickle! Look to your gathering there, Goodman Filcher.

FILCHER.

I warrant you, sir.

LEATHERHEAD.

And there come any gentlefolks, take twopence a piece, Sharkwell.

SHARKWELL.

I warrant you, Sir, threepence an' we can. [*Exeunt.*]

[V.ii] *The* Justice *comes in like a porter.*

JUSTICE OVERDO.

This later disguise, I have borrow'd of a porter, shall carry me out to all my great and good ends; which, however interrupted, were never destroyed in me: neither is

---

2. *invention*] work of imagination.

4–5. *carwhitchs*] quibbles.

8. *Pod*] Jonson's marginal note: *"Pod was a Master of Motions before him."*

9. *Ninive*] Nineveh.

11–12. *Shrove Tuesday*] when the apprentices annually wrecked brothels.

15. *projects*] designs (cf. V.ii.10). 18. *mickle*] great.

the hour of my severity yet come, to reveal myself, wherein, cloud-like, I will break out in rain and hail, lightning and thunder, upon the head of enormity. Two main works I have to prosecute: first, one is to invent some satisfaction for the poor, kind wretch, who is out of his wits for my sake; and yonder I see him coming; I will walk aside, and project for it.

[*Enter*] Winwife, Grace.

WINWIFE.

I wonder where Tom Quarlous is, that he returns not; it may be he is struck in here to seek us.

GRACE.

See, here's our madman again.

[*Enter*] Quarlous, Purecraft. Quarlous *in the habit of the madman is mistaken by* Mistress Purecraft.

QUARLOUS [*aside*].

I have made myself as like him, as his gown and cap will give me leave.

PURECRAFT.

Sir, I love you, and would be glad to be mad with you in truth.

WINWIFE.

How! my widow in love with a madman?

PURECRAFT.

Verily, I can be as mad in spirit, as you.

QUARLOUS.

By whose warrant? Leave your canting. Gentlewoman, have I found you? (Save ye, quit ye, and multiply ye.) Where's your book? 'Twas a sufficient name I mark'd, let me see't, be not afraid to shew't me.

He desires to see the book of Mistress Grace.

GRACE.

What would you with it, sir?

QUARLOUS.

Mark it again, and again, at your service.

---

20. *canting*] pious jargon.

GRACE.

Here it is, sir, this was it you mark'd.

QUARLOUS.

Palemon? Fare you well, fare you well.

WINWIFE.

How, Palemon!

GRACE.

Yes, faith, he has discover'd it to you, now, and therefore 'twere vain to disguise it longer; I am yours, sir, by the benefit of your fortune.

WINWIFE.

And you have him, mistress, believe it, that shall never give you cause to repent her benefit, but make you rather to think that, in this choice, she had both her eyes.

GRACE.

I desire to put it to no danger of protestation.

[*Exeunt* Grace *and* Winwife.]

QUARLOUS.

Palemon, the word, and Winwife the man?

PURECRAFT.

Good sir, vouchsafe a yoke-fellow in your madness; shun not one of the sanctified sisters, that would draw with you, in truth.

QUARLOUS.

Away, you are a herd of hypocritical proud ignorants, rather wild, than mad. Fitter for woods, and the society of beasts, than houses, and the congregation of men. You are the second part of the society of canters, outlaws to order and discipline, and the only privileg'd church-robbers of Christendom. Let me alone. Palemon, the word, and Winwife the man?

PURECRAFT [*aside*].

I must uncover myself unto him, or I shall never enjoy him, for all the cunning men's promises. [*to him*] Good sir, hear me, I am worth six thousand pound; my love to you is become my rack; I'll tell you all, and the truth, since you hate the hypocrisy of the parti-colored brotherhood. These seven years, I have been a willful holy widow only to draw feasts and gifts from my entangled suitors:

I am also by office, an assisting sister of the deacons, and a devourer, instead of a distributor of the alms. I am a special maker of marriages for our decayed brethren with our rich widows; for a third part of their wealth, when they are married, for the relief of the poor elect: as also our poor handsome young virgins with our wealthy bachelors, or widowers; to make them steal from their husbands, when I have confirmed them in the faith, and got all put into their custodies. And if I ha' not my bargain, they may sooner turn a scolding drab into a silent minister, than make me leave pronouncing reprobation, and damnation unto them. Our elder, Zeal-of-the-land, would have had me, but I know him to be the capital knave of the land, making himself rich by being made feoffee in trust to deceased brethren, and coz'ning their heirs by swearing the absolute gift of their inheritance. And thus, having eas'd my conscience, and utter'd my heart, with the tongue of my love: enjoy all my deceits together, I beseech you. I should not have revealed this to you, but that in time I think you are mad; and I hope you'll think me so too, sir!

QUARLOUS.

Stand aside, I'll answer you, presently.

He considers with himself of it.

Why should not I marry this six thousand pound, now I think on't? And a good trade too, that she has beside, ha? The tother wench, Winwife is sure of; there's no expectation for me there! Here I may make myself some saver; yet, if she continue mad, there's the question. It is money that I want; why should I not marry the money, when 'tis offer'd me? I have a license and all, it is but razing out one name, and putting in another. There's no playing

---

63–64. *silent minister*] term applied to those excommunicated for not complying with canons approved in 1604 by the Hampton Court Conference.

68. *feoffee in trust*] a trustee invested with a freehold estate.

73. *in time*] at a suitable time?

79. *make . . . saver*] compensate for loss (a gaming term).

with a man's fortune. I am resolv'd! I were truly mad, an' I would not! [*to her*] Well, come your ways, follow me, an' you will be mad, I'll show you a warrant!

He takes her along with him.

PURECRAFT.

Most zealously, it is that I zealously desire.

The Justice *calls him.*

JUSTICE OVERDO.

Sir, let me speak with you.

QUARLOUS.

By whose warrant?

JUSTICE OVERDO.

The warrant that you tender, and respect so; Justice Overdo's! I am the man, friend Trouble-All, though thus disguis'd (as the careful magistrate ought) for the good of the republic, in the Fair, and the weeding out of enormity. Do you want a house or meat, or drink, or clothes? Speak whatsoever it is, it shall be supplied you; what want you?

QUARLOUS.

Nothing but your warrant.

JUSTICE OVERDO.

My warrant? For what?

QUARLOUS.

To be gone, sir.

JUSTICE OVERDO.

Nay, I pray thee stay, I am serious, and have not many words, nor much time to exchange with thee; think what may do thee good.

QUARLOUS.

Your hand and seal, will do me a great deal of good; nothing else in the whole Fair, that I know.

JUSTICE OVERDO.

If it were to any end, thou should'st have it willingly.

QUARLOUS.

Why, it will satisfy me, that's end enough, to look on; an' you will not gi' it me, let me go.

JUSTICE OVERDO.

Alas! thou shalt ha' it presently: I'll but step into the scrivener's, hereby, and bring it. Do not go away.

The Justice *goes out.*

QUARLOUS [*aside*].

Why, this madman's shape will prove a very fortunate one, I think! Can a ragged robe produce these effects? If this be the wise Justice, and he bring me his hand, I shall go near to make some use on't.

[Justice] *returns.*

He is come already!

JUSTICE OVERDO.

Look thee! here is my hand and seal, Adam Overdo; if there be anything to be written, above in the paper, that thou want'st now, or at any time hereafter, think on't; it is my deed, I deliver it so; can your friend write?

QUARLOUS.

Her hand for a witness, and all is well.

JUSTICE OVERDO.

With all my heart.

He urgeth Mistress Purecraft.

QUARLOUS [*aside*].

Why should not I ha' the conscience to make this a bond of a thousand pound, now? or what I would else?

JUSTICE OVERDO.

Look you, there it is; and I deliver it as my deed again.

QUARLOUS.

Let us now proceed in madness. *He takes her in with him.*

JUSTICE OVERDO.

Well, my conscience is much eas'd; I ha' done my part; though it doth him no good, yet Adam hath offer'd satisfaction! The sting is removed from hence: poor man, he is much alter'd with his affliction, it has brought him low!

113.1. *returns*] *and returns. F margin.*

---

121. *conscience*] sound judgment.

Now, for my other work, reducing the young man I have follow'd so long in love, from the brink of his bane to the center of safety. Here, or in some such like vain place, I shall be sure to find him. I will wait the good time.

[V.iii] [*Enter*] Cokes, Sharkwell, Filcher.

COKES.
How now? What's here to do? Friend, art thou the master of the monuments?

SHARKWELL.
'Tis a motion, an't please your worship.

JUSTICE OVERDO [*aside*].
My fantastical brother-in-law, Master Bartholomew Cokes!

COKES.
A motion, what's that?

He reads the bill.

"The ancient modern history of *Hero and Leander,* otherwise called *The Touchstone of True Love,* with as true a trial of friendship, between Damon and Pythias, two faithful friends o' the Bankside" Pretty i' faith, what's the meaning on't? Is't an interlude? or what is't?

FILCHER.
Yes, sir; please you come near, we'll take your money within.

COKES.
Back with these children; they do so follow me up and down. *The boys o' the Fair follow him.*

[*Enter*] Littlewit.

LITTLEWIT.
By your leave, friend.

FILCHER.
You must pay, sir, an' you go in.

---

129. *reducing*] bringing back.

[V.iii]

1–2. *master . . . monuments*] phrase suggests the guide who took people around Westminster Abbey.

10. *interlude*] farce.

LITTLEWIT.

Who, I? I perceive thou know'st not me: call the master o' the motion.

SHARKWELL.

What, do you not know the author, fellow Filcher? You must take no money of him; he must come in *gratis:* Master Littlewit is a voluntary; he is the author.

LITTLEWIT.

Peace, speak not too loud, I would not have any notice taken, that I am the author, till we see how it passes.

COKES.

Master Littlewit, how dost thou?

LITTLEWIT.

Master Cokes! you are exceeding well met: what, in your doublet and hose, without a cloak or a hat?

COKES.

I would I might never stir, as I am an honest man, and by that fire; I have lost all i' the Fair, and all my acquaintance too; didst thou meet anybody that I know, Master Littlewit? My man Numps, or my sister Overdo, or Mistress Grace? Pray thee, Master Littlewit, lend me some money to see the interlude, here. I'll pay thee again, as I am a gentleman. If thou'lt but carry me home, I have money enough there.

LITTLEWIT.

O, sir, you shall command it; what, will a crown serve you?

COKES.

I think it will. What do we pay for coming in, fellows?

FILCHER.

Twopence, sir.

COKES.

Twopence? there's twelvepence, friend; nay, I am a gallant, as simple as I look now, if you see me with my man about me, and my artillery, again.

37. will] F_3; well *F*.

---

21. *voluntary*] a volunteer, who usually served without pay.

LITTLEWIT.

Your man was i' the stocks, e'en now, sir.

COKES.

Who, Numps?

LITTLEWIT.

Yes, faith.

COKES.

For what, i' faith? I am glad o' that; remember to tell me on't anon; I have enough, now! What manner of matter is this, Master Littlewit? What kind of actors ha' you? Are they good actors?

LITTLEWIT.

Pretty youths, sir, all children both old and young, here's the master of 'em—

[*Enter*] Leatherhead.

LEATHERHEAD.

(Call me not Leatherhead, but Lantern.)

Leatherhead *whispers to* Littlewit.

LITTLEWIT.

Master Lantern, that gives light to the business.

COKES.

In good time, sir, I would fain see 'em, I would be glad to drink with the young company; which is the tiring-house?

LEATHERHEAD.

Troth sir, our tiring-house is somewhat little; we are but beginners, yet, pray pardon us; you cannot go upright in't.

COKES.

No? Not now my hat is off? What would you have done with me, if you had had me, feather and all, as I was once today? Ha' you none of your pretty impudent boys, now, to bring stools, fill tobacco, fetch ale, and beg money, as they have at other houses? Let me see some o'

53–54. glad to drink] *W.*; glad drinke *F.*

---

51. (*Call . . . Lantern*)] to prevent his being recognized by Cokes; cf. III.vi.132–133.

your actors.

LITTLEWIT.

Show him 'em, show him 'em. Master Lantern, this is a gentleman, that is a favorer of the quality.

JUSTICE OVERDO [*aside*].

Aye, the favoring of this licentious quality is the consumption of many a young gentleman; a pernicious enormity.

COKES.

What, do they live in baskets?

LEATHERHEAD.

They do lie in a basket, sir, they are o' the small players.

He brings them out in a basket.

COKES.

These be players minors, indeed. Do you call these players?

LEATHERHEAD.

They are actors, sir, and as good as any, none disprais'd, for dumb shows: indeed, I am the mouth of 'em all!

COKES.

Thy mouth will hold 'em all. I think, one Taylor would go near to beat all this company, with a hand bound behind him.

LITTLEWIT.

Aye, and eat 'em all, too, an' they were in cake-bread.

COKES.

I thank you for that, Master Littlewit, a good jest! Which is your Burbage now?

LEATHERHEAD.

What mean you by that, sir?

---

65. *quality*] acting profession.

74. *mouth*] interpreter.

75. *Taylor*] (1) John Taylor, the Water Poet, who entertained the audience at the Hope on October 7, 1614; (2) Joseph Taylor, an actor with Lady Elizabeth's men in 1614 and possibly in the cast of this play; (3) tailors as proverbially timid.

78. *eat 'em*] tailors were supposedly greedy.

80. *Burbage*] an actor (1573–1619) especially noted for tragic roles.

COKES.

Your best actor. Your Field?

LITTLEWIT.

Good, i' faith! You are even with me, sir.

LEATHERHEAD.

This is he that acts young Leander, sir. He is extremely belov'd of the womenkind, they do so affect his action, the green gamesters that come here; and this is lovely Hero; this with the beard, Damon; and this, pretty Pythias: this is the ghost of King Dionysius in the habit of a scrivener: as you shall see anon, at large.

COKES.

Well they are a civil company, I like 'em for that; they offer not to fleer, nor jeer, nor break jests, as the great players do: and then, there goes not so much charge to the feasting of 'em, or making 'em drunk, as to the other, by reason of their littleness. Do they use to play perfect? Are they never fluster'd?

LEATHERHEAD.

No, sir, I thank my industry and policy for it; they are as well-govern'd a company, though I say it—and here is young Leander, is as proper an actor of his inches; and shakes his head like an ostler.

COKES.

But do you play it according to the printed book? I have read that.

LEATHERHEAD.

By no means, sir.

91. jeer] geere *F.*

---

82. *Field*] Nathan Field (1587–1619), actor, dramatist, friend of Jonson, probably in the cast of this play.

86. *green gamesters*] loose women (cf. IV.v.91–92).

88–89. *habit of a scrivener*] a gown with facings of fox fur and lambskin.

91. *fleer*] laugh scornfully.

99. *like an ostler*] perhaps alluding to the actor William Ostler of the King's Men; his head may have shaken when he acted (H.S.).

100. *printed book*] Marlowe's *Hero and Leander,* from whose first four lines Leatherhead quotes in ll. 105–107.

COKES.

No? How then?

LEATHERHEAD.

A better way, sir; that is too learned and poetical for our audience; what do they know what Hellespont is? "Guilty of true love's blood?" Or what Abydos is? Or "the other Sestos hight?"

COKES.

Th' art i' the right, I do not know myself.

LEATHERHEAD.

No, I have entreated Master Littlewit, to take a little pains to reduce it to a more familiar strain for our people.

COKES.

How, I pray thee, good Master Littlewit?

LITTLEWIT.

It pleases him to make a matter of it, sir. But there is no such matter I assure you: I have only made it a little easy, and modern for the times, sir, that's all; as, for the Hellespont, I imagine our Thames here; and then Leander I make a dyer's son, about Puddle-wharf; and Hero a wench o' the Bank-side, who going over one morning, to old Fish-street, Leander spies her land at Trig-stairs, and falls in love with her: now do I introduce Cupid, having metamorphos'd himself into a drawer, and he strikes Hero in love with a pint of sherry; and other pretty passages there are, o' the friendship, that will delight you, sir, and please you of judgment.

COKES.

I'll be sworn they shall; I am in love with the actors already, and I'll be allied to them presently. (They respect gentlemen, these fellows.) Hero shall be my fairing: but, which of my fairings? Le' me see—i' faith, my fiddle! and Leander my fiddlestick: then Damon, my drum; and

---

114. *modern*] commonplace.

116. *Puddle-wharf*] a water gate into the Thames near Paul's Stairs where horses used to be watered (Stow, II, 13).

118. *old Fish-street*] center of fish trade.

118. *Trig-stairs*] at the end of Trig Lane, next to Puddle-wharf.

126. *fairing*] a present bought at a fair.

Pythias, my pipe, and the ghost of Dionysius, my hobby-horse. All fitted.

[V.iv] [*Enter*] *to them* Winwife, Grace.

WINWIFE.

Look, yonder's your Cokes gotten in among his play-fellows; I thought we could not miss him, at such a spectacle.

GRACE.

Let him alone, he is so busy, he will never spy us.

LEATHERHEAD.

Nay, good sir. Cokes *is handling the puppets.*

COKES.

I warrant thee, I will not hurt her, fellow; what, dost think me uncivil? I pray thee be not jealous: I am toward a wife.

LITTLEWIT.

Well, good Master Lantern, make ready to begin, that I may fetch my wife, and look you be perfect; you undo me else, i' my reputation.

LEATHERHEAD.

I warrant you, sir, do not you breed too great an expectation of it, among your friends: that's the only hurter of these things.

LITTLEWIT.

No, no, no. [*Exit.*]

COKES.

I'll stay here, and see; pray thee let me see.

WINWIFE.

How diligent and troublesome he is!

GRACE.

The place becomes him, methinks.

JUSTICE OVERDO [*aside*].

My ward, Mistress Grace, in the company of a stranger? I doubt I shall be compell'd to discover myself, before my time!

[V.iv]

7. *toward*] in prospect of.

17. *troublesome*] laborious, painstaking.

[*Enter*] Knockem, Edgworth, Win, Whit, Mistress Overdo.

The door-keepers speak.

FILCHER.
Twopence apiece, gentlemen, an excellent motion.

KNOCKEM.
Shall we have fine fireworks, and good vapors?

SHARKWELL.
Yes, captain, and waterworks, too.

WHIT.
I pre dee, take a care o' dy shmall lady, there, Edgworth; I will look to dish tall lady myself.

LEATHERHEAD.
Welcome, gentlemen, welcome, gentlemen.

WHIT.
Pre dee, mashter o' de monshtersh, help a very sick lady, here, to a chair, to shit in.

LEATHERHEAD.
Presently, sir.

They bring Mistress Overdo *a chair.*

WHIT.
Good fait now, Urs'la's ale and *aqua vitae* ish to blame for't; shit down, shweetheart, shit down, and shleep a little.

EDGWORTH.
Madam, you are very welcome hither.

KNOCKEM.
Yes, and you shall see very good vapors.

JUSTICE OVERDO [*aside*].
Here is my care come! I like to see him in so good company; and yet I wonder that persons of such fashion, should resort hither! *By* Edgworth.

EDGWORTH.
This is a very private house, madam.

---

26. *tall*] fine.
31. *aqua vitae*] ardent spirits (like whiskey or brandy).
38. S.D. *By*] with reference to.

LEATHERHEAD.

Will it please your ladyship sit, madam?

The cutpurse courts Mistress Littlewit.

WIN.

Yes, good man. They do so all-to-be-madam me, I think they think me a very lady!

EDGWORTH.

What else, madam?

WIN.

Must I put off my mask to him?

EDGWORTH.

O, by no means.

WIN.

How should my husband know me, then?

KNOCKEM.

Husband? an idle vapor; he must not know you, nor you him; there's the true vapor.

JUSTICE OVERDO [*aside*].

Yea, I will observe more of this. [*to Whit*] Is this a lady, friend?

WHIT.

Aye, and dat is anoder lady, shweetheart; if dou hasht a mind to 'em give me twelvepence from tee, and dou shalt have eder-oder on 'em!

JUSTICE OVERDO [*aside*].

Aye? This will prove my chiefest enormity: I will follow this.

EDGWORTH.

Is not this a finer life, lady, than to be clogg'd with a husband?

WIN.

Yes, a great deal. When will they begin, trow, in the name o' the motion?

EDGWORTH.

By and by, madam; they stay but for company.

---

41. *all-to-be-madam*] always call me madam.
53. *eder-oder*] one or the other of two.

KNOCKEM.

Do you hear, puppet-master, these are tedious vapors; when begin you?

LEATHERHEAD.

We stay but for Master Littlewit, the author, who is gone for his wife; and we begin presently.

WIN.

That's I, that's I.

EDGWORTH.

That was you, lady; but now you are no such poor thing.

KNOCKEM.

Hang the author's wife, a running vapor! Here be ladies, will stay for ne'er a Delia o' 'em all.

WHIT.

But hear me now, here ish one o' de ladish, ashleep; stay till she but vake, man.

[*Enter*] *to them* Wasp. *The door-keepers again.*

WASP.

How now, friends? What's here to do?

FILCHER.

Twopence a piece, sir, the best motion, in the Fair.

WASP.

I believe you lie; if you do, I'll have my money again, and beat you.

WINWIFE.

Numps is come!

WASP.

Did you see a master of mine come in here, a tall young squire of Harrow o' the Hill, Master Bartholomew Cokes?

FILCHER.

I think there be such a one, within.

WASP.

Look he be, you were best: but it is very likely: I wonder I found him not at all the rest. I ha' been at the Eagle, and the Black Wolf, and the Bull with the five legs and two pizzles (he was a calf at Uxbridge Fair, two years

---

68. *Delia*] the lady of Samuel Daniel's *Sonnets* (1592).

agone), and at the Dogs that dance the morris, and the Hare o' the tabor; and miss'd him at all these! Sure this must needs be some fine sight, that holds him so, if it have him.

COKES.

Come, come, are you ready now?

LEATHERHEAD.

Presently, sir.

WASP.

Hoyday, he's at work in his doublet and hose; do you hear, sir? Are you employ'd, that you are bareheaded, and so busy?

COKES.

Hold your peace, Numps; you ha' been i' the stocks, I hear.

WASP.

Does he know that? Nay, then the date of my authority is out; I must think no longer to reign, my government is at an end. He that will correct another, must want fault in himself.

WINWIFE.

Sententious Numps! I never heard so much from him, before.

LEATHERHEAD.

Sure, Master Littlewit will not come; please you take your place, sir, we'll begin.

COKES.

I pray thee do, mine ears long to be at it; and my eyes too. O Numps, i' the stocks, Numps? Where's your sword, Numps?

WASP.

I pray you intend your game, sir, let me alone.

COKES.

Well then, we are quit for all. Come, sit down, Numps;

96–97. fault in himself] *F*; fault himselfe *reset F*.

---

89. *Hoyday*] hey-day (exclam. of surprise).
105. *intend*] attend to.

I'll interpret to thee: did you see Mistress Grace? It's no matter, neither, now I think on't, tell me anon.

WINWIFE.

A great deal of love, and care, he expresses.

GRACE.

Alas! would you have him to express more than he has? That were tyranny.

COKES.

Peace, ho; now, now.

LEATHERHEAD.

Gentles, that no longer your expectations may wander,
Behold our chief actor, amorous Leander,
With a great deal of cloth lapp'd about him like a scarf,
For he yet serves his father, a dyer at Puddle-wharf,
Which place we'll make bold with, to call it our Abydus,
As the Bankside is our Sestos, and let it not be denied us.
Now, as he is beating, to make the dye take the fuller,
Who chances to come by, but fair Hero, in a sculler;
And seeing Leander's naked leg, and goodly calf,
Cast at him, from the boat, a sheep's eye, and a half.
Now she is landed, and the sculler come back;
By and by, you shall see what Leander doth lack.

PUPPET LEANDER.

Cole, Cole, old Cole.

LEATHERHEAD.

That is the sculler's name without control.

PUPPET LEANDER.

Cole, Cole, I say, Cole.

LEATHERHEAD.

We do hear you.

110. to express] *F*; expresse *reset F*. 128. *We . . . you*] *not ital. in F.*

---

113. *Gentles*] the puppet play mixes two of the most popular Renaissance stories and possibly echoes well-known Elizabethan renderings of them: Marlowe's *Hero and Leander* and Richard Edwardes' *Damon and Pithias* (1571).

119. *fuller*] more thoroughly.

122. *sheep's eye*] amorous look.

125. *Cole*] conventional name for a pander.

PUPPET LEANDER.

Old Cole.

LEATHERHEAD.

Old Cole? Is the dyer turn'd collier? How do you sell?

PUPPET LEANDER.

A pox o' your manners, kiss my hole here, and smell.

LEATHERHEAD.

Kiss your hole, and smell? There's manners indeed.

PUPPET LEANDER.

Why, Cole, I say, Cole.

LEATHERHEAD.

It's the sculler you need!

PUPPET LEANDER.

Aye, and be hang'd.

LEATHERHEAD.

Be hang'd; look you yonder,
Old Cole, you must go hang with Master Leander.

PUPPET COLE.

Where is he?

PUPPET LEANDER.

Here, Cole, what fairest of fairs
Was that fare, that thou landest but now at Trig-stairs?

COKES.

What was that, fellow? Pray thee tell me, I scarce understand 'em.

LEATHERHEAD.

Leander does ask, sir, what fairest of fairs
Was the fare that he landed, but now, at Trig-stairs?

PUPPET COLE.

It is lovely Hero.

PUPPET LEANDER.

Nero?

PUPPET COLE.

No, Hero.

140. *at*] F_3; *a F.* 144. *that he*] *H.S.; thhe F; he* F_3.

---

130. *collier*] a term of abuse: colliers were reputed to cheat their customers.

LEATHERHEAD.

It is Hero
Of the Bankside, he saith, to tell you truth without erring,
Is come over into Fish-street to eat some fresh herring,
Leander says no more, but as fast as he can,
Gets on all his best clothes; and will after to the Swan.

COKES.

Most admirable good, is't not?

LEATHERHEAD.

Stay, sculler.

PUPPET COLE.

What say you?

LEATHERHEAD.

You must stay for Leander, and carry him to the wench.

PUPPET COLE.

You rogue, I am no pander.

COKES.

He says he is no pander. 'Tis a fine language; I understand it now.

LEATHERHEAD.

Are you no pander, Goodman Cole? Here's no man says
you are,
You'll grow a hot Cole, it seems, pray you stay for your fare.

PUPPET COLE.

Will he come away?

LEATHERHEAD.

What do you say?

PUPPET COLE.

I'd ha' him come away.

LEATHERHEAD.

Would you ha' Leander come away? Why 'pray, sir, stay.
You are angry, Goodman Cole; I believe the fair maid
Came over wi' you o' trust: tell us, sculler, are you paid?

PUPPET COLE.

Yes, Goodman Hogrubber o' Pickt-hatch.

LEATHERHEAD.

How, Hogrubber, o' Pickt-hatch?

---

168. *Hogrubber*] swineherd. 168. *Pickt-hatch*] haunt of prostitutes.

PUPPET COLE.

Aye, Hogrubber o' Pickt-hatch. Take you that.

The Puppet *strikes him over the pate.*

LEATHERHEAD.

O, my head!

PUPPET COLE.

Harm watch, harm catch.

COKES.

Harm watch, harm catch, he says: very good i' faith, the Sculler had like to ha' knock'd you, sirrah.

LEATHERHEAD.

Yes, but that his fare call'd him away.

PUPPET LEANDER.

Row apace, row apace, row, row, row, row, row.

LEATHERHEAD.

You are knavishly loaden, sculler, take heed where you go.

PUPPET COLE.

Knave i' your face, Goodman Rogue.

PUPPET LEANDER.

Row, row, row, row, row, row.

COKES.

He said "knave i' your face," friend.

LEATHERHEAD.

Aye, sir, I heard him. But there's no talking to these watermen, they will ha' the last word.

COKES.

God's my life! I am not allied to the sculler, yet; he shall be Dauphin my boy. But my Fiddlestick does fiddle in and out too much; I pray thee speak to him on't; tell him, I would have him tarry in my sight, more.

LEATHERHEAD.

I pray you be content; you'll have enough on him, sir.
Now, gentles, I take it, here is none of you so stupid,
But that you have heard of a little god of love, call'd Cupid.
Who out of kindness to Leander, hearing he but saw her,

---

184. *Dauphin my boy*] alluding to a ballad, now lost, quoted by Edgar in *Lear,* III.iv.100.

184. *Fiddlestick*] Leander (cf. V.iii.128).

This present day and hour, doth turn himself to a drawer.
And because he would have their first meeting to be merry,
He strikes Hero in love to him, with a pint of sherry.
Which he tells her, from amorous Leander is sent her,
Who after him, into the room of Hero, doth venter.

PUPPET JONAS.

A pint of sack, score a pint of sack, i' the Coney.

Puppet Leander *goes into* Mistress Hero's *room.*

COKES.

Sack? You said but e'en now it should be sherry.

PUPPET JONAS.

Why so it is; sherry, sherry, sherry.

COKES.

"Sherry, sherry, sherry." By my troth he makes me merry. I must have a name for Cupid, too. Let me see, thou mightst help me now, an' thou wouldest, Numps, at a dead lift, but thou art dreaming o' the stocks, still! Do not think on't, I have forgot it: 'tis but a nine days' wonder, man; let it not trouble thee.

WASP.

I would the stocks were about your neck, sir; condition I hung by the heels in them, till the wonder were off from you, with all my heart.

COKES.

Well said, resolute Numps: but hark you friend, where is the friendship, all this while, between my drum, Damon, and my pipe, Pythias?

LEATHERHEAD.

You shall see by and by, sir!

COKES.

You think my hobbyhorse is forgotten, too; no, I'll see

---

196. *the Coney*] name of a room in the tavern.

197. *Sack . . . sherry*] a stupid remark since sack was the general name for all white wines.

202. *dead lift*] a last extremity (Nares).

205. *condition*] on condition that.

212. *hobbyhorse is forgotten*] another of Cokes's reference to a popular ballad; cf. *Hamlet,* III.ii.146.

'em all enact before I go; I shall not know which to love best, else.

KNOCKEM.

This gallant has interrupting vapors, troublesome vapors, Whit, puff with him.

WHIT.

No, I pre dee, captain, let him alone. He is a child i' faith, la.

LEATHERHEAD.

Now, gentles, to the friends, who in number are two,
And lodg'd in that ale-house, in which fair Hero does do.
Damon (for some kindness done him the last week)
Is come fair Hero, in Fish-street, this morning to seek:
Pythias does smell the knavery of the meeting,
And now you shall see their true friendly greeting.

PUPPET PYTHIAS.

You whore-masterly slave, you.

COKES.

Whore-masterly slave you? Very friendly, and familiar, that.

PUPPET DAMON.

Whore-master i' thy face,
Thou hast lien with her thyself, I'll prove't i' this place.

COKES.

Damon says Pythias has lien with her, himself, he'll prove't in this place.

LEATHERHEAD.

They are whore-masters both, sir, that's a plain case.

PUPPET PYTHIAS.

You lie, like a rogue.

LEATHERHEAD.

Do I lie, like a rogue?

PUPPET PYTHIAS.

A pimp, and a scab.

LEATHERHEAD.

A pimp, and a scab?

---

216. *puff with*] "vapor," quarrel, act insolently.
235. *scab*] scoundrel.

I say between you, you have both but one drab.

PUPPET DAMON.

You lie again.

LEATHERHEAD.

Do I lie again?

PUPPET DAMON.

Like a rogue again.

LEATHERHEAD.

Like a rogue again?

PUPPET PYTHIAS.

And you are a pimp, again.

COKES.

And you are a pimp again, he says.

PUPPET DAMON.

And a scab, again.

COKES.

And a scab again, he says.

LEATHERHEAD.

And I say again, you are both whore-masters again,
And you have both but one drab again.

They fight.

PUPPETS DAMON, PYTHIAS.

Dost thou, dost thou, dost thou?

LEATHERHEAD.

What, both at once?

PUPPET PYTHIAS.

Down with him, Damon.

PUPPET DAMON.

Pink his guts, Pythias.

LEATHERHEAD.

What, so malicious?
Will ye murder me, masters both, i' mine own house?

COKES.

Ho! well acted my drum, well acted my pipe, well acted still.

WASP.

Well acted, with all my heart.

---

251. *Pink*] stab.

LEATHERHEAD.
Hold, hold your hands.

COKES.
Aye, both your hands, for my sake! for you ha' both done well.

PUPPET DAMON.
Gramercy, pure Pythias.

PUPPET PYTHIAS.
Gramercy, dear Damon.

COKES.
Gramercy to you both, my pipe, and my drum.

PUPPETS DAMON, PYTHIAS.
Come now, we'll together to breakfast to Hero.

LEATHERHEAD.
'Tis well, you can now go to breakfast to Hero,
You have given me my breakfast, with ohone and 'honero.

COKES.
How is't, friend, ha' they hurt thee?

LEATHERHEAD.
O no!
Between you and I, sir, we do but make show.
Thus, gentles, you perceive, without any denial,
'Twixt Damon and Pythias here, friendship's true trial.
Though hourly they quarrel thus, and roar each with other,
They fight you no more, than does brother with brother.
But friendly together, at the next man they meet,
They let fly their anger, as here you might see't.

COKES.
Well, we have seen't, and thou hast felt it, whatsoever thou sayest. What's next? What's next?

LEATHERHEAD.
This while young Leander, with fair Hero is drinking,
And Hero grown drunk, to any man's thinking!
Yet was it not three pints of sherry could flaw her,

265. *me my*] F_3; *mmy F.*

---

260. *pure*] good.
265. *ohone and 'honero*] alas! (apparently a ballad refrain).
279. *flaw her*] make her drunk.

Till Cupid, distinguish'd like Jonas the drawer,
From under his apron, where his lechery lurks,
Put love in her sack. Now mark how it works.

PUPPET HERO.
O Leander, Leander, my dear, my dear Leander,
I'll for ever be thy goose, so thou'lt be my gander.

COKES.
Excellently well said, fiddle, she'll ever be his goose, so he'll be her gander: was't not so?

LEATHERHEAD.
Yes, sir, but mark his answer, now.

PUPPET LEANDER.
And sweetest of geese, before I go to bed,
I'll swim o'er the Thames, my goose, thee to tread.

COKES.
Brave! he will swim o'er the Thames, and tread his goose, tonight, he says.

LEATHERHEAD.
Aye, peace, sir, they'll be angry, if they hear you eavesdropping, now they are setting their match.

PUPPET LEANDER.
But lest the Thames should be dark, my goose, my dear friend,
Let thy window be provided of a candle's end.

PUPPET HERO.
Fear not, my gander, I protest, I should handle
My matters very ill, if I had not a whole candle.

PUPPET LEANDER.
Well then, look to't, and kiss me to boot.

LEATHERHEAD.
Now, here come the friends again, Pythias and Damon,
And under their cloaks, they have of bacon, a gammon.

Damon *and* Pythias *enter.*

PUPPET PYTHIAS.
Drawer, fill some wine here.

292. they'll] F_3; the'll *F*.

---

289. *tread*] copulate with.
293. *setting their match*] appointing a time to meet.

LEATHERHEAD.

How, some wine there?
There's company already, sir, pray forbear!

PUPPET DAMON.

'Tis Hero.

LEATHERHEAD.

Yes, but she will not be taken,
After sack, and fresh herring, with your Dunmow-bacon.

PUPPET PYTHIAS.

You lie, it's Westfabian.

LEATHERHEAD.

Westphalian you should say.

PUPPET DAMON.

If you hold not your peace, you are a coxcomb, I would say.

Leander *and* Hero *are kissing.*

PUPPET PYTHIAS.

What's here? What's here? Kiss, kiss, upon kiss.

LEATHERHEAD.

Aye, wherefore should they not? What harm is in this?
'Tis Mistress Hero.

PUPPET DAMON.

Mistress Hero's a whore.

LEATHERHEAD.

Is she a whore? Keep you quiet, or sir knave out of door.

PUPPET DAMON.

Knave out of door?

PUPPET HERO.

Yes, knave, out of door.

PUPPET DAMON.

Whore out of door.

302–303. *How . . . forbear*] *not ital. in F.*

310. S.P. PUPPET PYTHIAS] PVP *F.*

---

306. *Dunmow-bacon*] given to any couple who could convince a jury of six maidens and six bachelors of Little Dunmow in Essex that they had spent the first year of married life without quarreling or wishing they had waited.

308. *Westphalian*] still famous for hams.

Here the Puppets *quarrel and fall together by the ears.*

PUPPET HERO.
I say, knave, out of door.

PUPPET DAMON.
I say, whore, out of door.

PUPPET PYTHIAS.
Yea, so say I too.

PUPPET HERO.
Kiss the whore o' the arse.

LEATHERHEAD.
Now you ha' something to do: you must kiss her o' the arse she says.

PUPPETS DAMON, PYTHIAS.
So we will, so we will. [*They kick her.*]

PUPPET HERO.
O my haunches, O my haunches, hold, hold.

LEATHERHEAD.
Stand'st thou still?
Leander, where art thou? Stand'st thou still like a sot,
And not offer'st to break both their heads with a pot?
See who's at thine elbow there! Puppet Jonas and Cupid.

PUPPET JONAS.
Upon 'em, Leander, be not so stupid.

They fight.

PUPPET LEANDER.
You goat-bearded slave!

PUPPET DAMON.
You whore-master knave.

PUPPET LEANDER.
Thou art a whore-master.

PUPPET JONAS.
Whore-masters all.

LEATHERHEAD.
See, Cupid with a word has ta'en up the brawl.

KNOCKEM.
These be fine vapors!

COKES.
By this good day they fight bravely! Do they not, Numps?

WASP.

Yes, they lack'd but you to be their second, all this while.

LEATHERHEAD.

This tragical encounter, falling out thus to busy us,
It raises up the ghost of their friend Dionysius:
Not like a monarch, but the master of a school,
In a scrivener's furr'd gown, which shows he is no fool.
For therein he hath wit enough to keep himself warm.
"O Damon," he cries, "and Pythias; what harm
Hath poor Dionysius done you in his grave,
That after his death, you should fall out thus, and rave,
And call amorous Leander whore-master knave?"

PUPPET DAMON.

I cannot, I will not, I promise you, endure it.

[V.v] [*Enter*] *to them* Busy.

BUSY.

Down with Dagon, down with Dagon; 'tis I, will no longer endure your profanations.

LEATHERHEAD.

What mean you, sir?

BUSY.

I will remove Dagon there, I say, that idol, that heathenish idol, that remains (as I may say) a beam, a very beam, not a beam of the sun, nor a beam of the moon, nor a beam of a balance, neither a house-beam, nor a weaver's beam, but a beam in the eye, in the eye of the brethren; a very great beam, an exceeding great beam; such as are your stage-players, rhymers, and morris-dancers, who have walked hand in hand, in contempt of the brethren and the cause, and been borne out by instruments, of no

---

340–341. *Dionysius . . . master of a school*] Dionysius, tyrant of Syracuse (367–343 B.C.), according to some accounts kept a school at Corinth after his abdication.

[V.v]

1. *Dagon*] god of the Philistines.

12. *instruments*] agents.

mean countenance.

LEATHERHEAD.

Sir, I present nothing, but what is licens'd by authority.

BUSY.

Thou art all license, even licentiousness itself, Shimei!

LEATHERHEAD.

I have the Master of the Revels' hand for't, sir.

BUSY.

The Master of Rebels' hand, thou hast; Satan's! Hold thy peace, thy scurrility, shut up thy mouth, thy profession is damnable, and in pleading for it, thou dost plead for Baal. I have long opened my mouth wide, and gaped, I have gaped as the oyster for the tide, after thy destruction: but cannot compass it by suit, or dispute; so that I look for a bickering, ere long, and then a battle.

KNOCKEM.

Good Banbury-vapors.

COKES.

Friend, you'd have an ill match on't, if you bicker with him here; though he be no man o' the fist, he has friends that will go to cuffs for him. Numps, will not you take our side?

EDGWORTH.

Sir, it shall not need; in my mind, he offers him a fairer course, to end it by disputation! Hast thou nothing to say for thyself, in defense of thy quality?

LEATHERHEAD.

Faith, sir, I am not well studied in these controversies, between the hypocrites and us. But here's one of my motion, Puppet Dionysius, shall undertake him, and I'll venture the cause on't.

COKES.

Who? My hobbyhorse? Will he dispute with him?

---

13. *countenance*] repute.

15. *Shimei*] the son of Gera who cursed David, stoned the Israelites, and was killed by Solomon (2 Samuel xvi:5–13).

16. *Master of the Revels*] licenser of plays.

20. *for Baal*] for heathen idols.

LEATHERHEAD.

Yes, sir, and make a hobby-ass of him, I hope.

COKES.

That's excellent! Indeed he looks like the best scholar of 'em all. Come, sir, you must be as good as your word, now.

BUSY.

I will not fear to make my spirit, and gifts known! Assist me, zeal; fill me, fill me, that is, make me full.

WINWIFE.

What a desperate, profane wretch is this! Is there any ignorance, or impudence, like his? To call his zeal to fill him against a puppet?

GRACE.

I know no fitter match, than a puppet to commit with an hypocrite!

BUSY.

First, I say unto thee, idol, thou hast no calling.

PUPPET DIONYSIUS.

You lie, I am call'd Dionysius.

LEATHERHEAD.

The motion says you lie, he is call'd Dionysius i' the matter, and to that calling he answers.

BUSY.

I mean no vocation, idol, no present lawful calling.

PUPPET DIONYSIUS.

Is yours a lawful calling?

LEATHERHEAD.

The motion asketh, if yours be a lawful calling?

BUSY.

Yes, mine is of the spirit.

PUPPET DIONYSIUS.

Then idol is a lawful calling.

LEATHERHEAD.

He says, then idol is a lawful calling! For you call'd him idol, and your calling is of the spirit.

45. S.P. GRACE] Spencer; Quarlous *F*, F_3, G., H.S.

---

45. *commit with*] fight with.

COKES.

Well disputed, hobbyhorse!

BUSY.

Take not part with the wicked, young gallant. He neigheth and hinnyeth, all is but hinnying sophistry. I call him idol again. Yet, I say, his calling, his profession is profane, it is profane, idol.

PUPPET DIONYSIUS.

It is not profane!

LEATHERHEAD.

It is not profane, he says.

BUSY.

It is profane.

PUPPET DIONYSIUS.

It is not profane.

BUSY.

It is profane.

PUPPET DIONYSIUS.

It is not profane.

LEATHERHEAD.

Well said, confute him with "not," still. You cannot bear him down with your bass noise, sir.

BUSY.

Nor he me, with his treble creaking, though he creak like the chariot wheels of Satan; I am zealous for the cause—

LEATHERHEAD.

As a dog for a bone.

BUSY.

And I say, it is profane, as being the page of Pride, and the waiting-woman of Vanity.

PUPPET DIONYSIUS.

Yea? What say you to your tire-women, then?

LEATHERHEAD.

Good.

---

60. *hinnyeth*] whinnies.
71. *creak*] speak querulously; grate shrilly.
76–78. *tire-women . . . feather-makers*] Puritans were often taunted because they prospered by selling the fancy dress they cursed others for wearing.

PUPPET DIONYSIUS.

Or feather-makers i' the Friars, that are o' your faction of faith? Are not they with their perukes, and their puffs, their fans, and their huffs, as much pages of Pride, and waiters upon Vanity? What say you? What say you? What say you?

BUSY.

I will not answer for them.

PUPPET DIONYSIUS.

Because you cannot, because you cannot. Is a bugle-maker a lawful calling? Or the confect-maker's (such you have there)? Or your French fashioner? You'd have all the sin within yourselves, would you not? Would you not?

BUSY.

No, Dagon.

PUPPET DIONYSIUS.

What then, Dagonet? Is a puppet worse than these?

BUSY.

Yes, and my main argument against you, is, that you are an abomination: for the male, among you, putteth on the apparel of the female, and the female of the male.

PUPPET DIONYSIUS.

You lie, you lie, you lie abominably.

COKES.

Good, by my troth, he has given him the lie thrice.

PUPPET DIONYSIUS.

It is your old stale argument against the players, but it will not hold against the puppets; for we have neither male nor female amongst us. And that thou may'st see, if thou wilt, like a malicious purblind zeal as thou art!

The Puppet *takes up his garment.*

84–85. *bugle-maker*] maker of glass beads.

85. *confect-maker's*] maker of sweetmeats.

86. *fashioner*] tailor.

89. *Dagonet*] King Arthur's fool.

91. *male*] cf. Deut. xxii:5 for the biblical prohibition against the sexes exchanging clothes; Prynne used this and other scriptural passages to argue that any man acting a woman's part in woman's dress was sinful (*Histriomastix* [1633], pp. 178–210).

EDGWORTH.

By my faith, there he has answer'd you, friend; by plain demonstration.

PUPPET DIONYSIUS.

Nay, I'll prove, against e'er a Rabbin of 'em all, that my standing is as lawful as his; that I speak by inspiration, as well as he; that I have as little to do with learning as he; and do scorn her helps as much as he.

BUSY.

I am confuted, the cause hath failed me.

PUPPET DIONYSIUS.

Then be converted, be converted.

LEATHERHEAD.

Be converted, I pray you, and let the play go on!

BUSY.

Let it go on. For I am changed, and will become a beholder with you!

COKES.

That's brave i' faith; thou hast carried it away, hobby-horse; on with the play!

The Justice *discovers himself.*

JUSTICE OVERDO.

Stay, now do I forbid, I Adam Overdo! Sit still, I charge you.

COKES.

What, my brother-i'-law!

GRACE.

My wise guardian!

EDGWORTH.

Justice Overdo!

JUSTICE OVERDO.

It is time, to take enormity by the forehead, and brand it; for I have discover'd enough.

[V.vi]

[*Enter*] *to them,* Quarlous *(like the madman),* Purecraft *(a while after).*

---

110. *carried it away*] won.

QUARLOUS.

Nay, come, mistress bride. You must do as I do, now. You must be mad with me, in truth. I have here Justice Overdo for it.

JUSTICE OVERDO.

Peace, good Trouble-All; come hither, and you shall trouble none. I will take the charge of you and your friend too; —you also, young man, shall be my care, stand there. *To the cutpurse and* Mistress Littlewit.

EDGWORTH.

Now, mercy upon me. *The rest are stealing away.*

KNOCKEM.

Would we were away, Whit; these are dangerous vapors; best fall off with our birds, for fear o' the cage.

JUSTICE OVERDO.

Stay, is not my name your terror?

WHIT.

Yesh, faith, man, and it ish for tat we would be gone, man.

[*Enter*] Littlewit.

LITTLEWIT.

O gentlemen! did you not see a wife of mine? I ha' lost my little wife, as I shall be trusted: my little pretty Win, I left her at the great woman's house in trust yonder, the pig-woman's, with Captain Jordan, and Captain Whit, very good men, and I cannot hear of her. Poor fool, I fear she's stepp'd aside. Mother, did you not see Win?

JUSTICE OVERDO.

If this grave matron be your mother, sir, stand by her, *et digito compesce labellum,* I may perhaps spring a wife for you, anon. Brother Bartholomew, I am sadly sorry, to see you so lightly given, and such a disciple of enormity; with your grave governor Humphrey: but stand

7. S.D.] *F prints in margin beside ll. 5–7.*

---

10. *cage*] prison.

19. *stepp'd aside*] gone astray.

20–21. *et . . . labellum*] Juvenal *Sat.* I. 160: "put your finger to your lip" (G. G. Ramsay).

21. *spring*] to cause a bird to rise from cover.

you both there, in the middle place; I will reprehend you in your course. Mistress Grace, let me rescue you out of the hands of the stranger.

WINWIFE.

Pardon me, sir, I am a kinsman of hers.

JUSTICE OVERDO.

Are you so? Of what name, sir?

WINWIFE.

Winwife, sir.

JUSTICE OVERDO.

Master Winwife? I hope you have won no wife of her, sir. If you have, I will examine the possibility of it, at fit leisure. Now, to my enormities: look upon me, O London! and see me, O Smithfield! the example of justice, and Mirror of Magistrates; the true top of formality, and scourge of enormity. Hearken unto my labors, and but observe my discoveries; and compare Hercules with me, if thou dar'st, of old; or Columbus; Magellan; or our countryman Drake of later times: stand forth you weeds of enormity, and spread. (*To* Busy) First, Rabbi Busy, thou super-lunatical hypocrite. (*To* Leatherhead) Next, thou other extremity, thou profane professor of puppetry, little better than poetry. (*To the horse-courser, and cutpurse*) Then thou strong debaucher, and seducer of youth; witness this easy and honest young man. (*Then* Captain Whit *and* Mistress Littlewit) Now thou esquire of dames, madams, and twelvepenny ladies: now my green madam herself, of the price. Let me unmask your ladyship.

LITTLEWIT.

O my wife, my wife, my wife!

JUSTICE OVERDO.

Is she your wife? *Redde te Harpocratem!*

Enter Trouble-All, Ursula, Nightingale.

40. S.D. (*To* Busy)] *all the stage directions here enclosed in parentheses are placed in the margin of the Folio.*

---

51. *Redde te Harpocratem*] "make yourself like Harpocrates," god of silence.

TROUBLE-ALL.

By your leave, stand by, my masters, be uncover'd.

URSULA.

O stay him, stay him, help to cry, Nightingale; my pan, my pan.

JUSTICE OVERDO.

What's the matter?

NIGHTINGALE.

He has stol'n Gammer Urs'la's pan.

TROUBLE-ALL.

Yes, and I fear no man but Justice Overdo.

JUSTICE OVERDO.

Urs'la? Where is she? O the sow of enormity, this! (*To* Ursula *and* Nightingale) Welcome, stand you there; you, songster, there.

URSULA.

An' please your worship, I am in no fault: a gentleman stripp'd him in my booth, and borrow'd his gown, and his hat; and he ran away with my goods, here, for it.

JUSTICE OVERDO (*to* Quarlous).

Then this is the true madman, and you are the enormity!

QUARLOUS.

You are i' the right, I am mad, but from the gown outward.

JUSTICE OVERDO.

Stand you there.

QUARLOUS.

Where you please, sir.

Mistress Overdo *is sick: and her husband is silenc'd.*

MRS. OVERDO.

O lend me a basin, I am sick, I am sick; where's Master Overdo? Bridget, call hither my Adam.

JUSTICE OVERDO.

How?

WHIT.

Dy very own wife, i' fait, worshipful Adam.

---

70. *Bridget*] a mistake of Jonson's for "Grace"? (H.S.).

MRS. OVERDO.

Will not my Adam come at me? Shall I see him no more then?

QUARLOUS.

Sir, why do you not go on with the enormity? Are you oppress'd with it? I'll help you: hark you, sir, i' your ear: your "innocent young man," you have ta'en such care of, all this day, is a cutpurse, that hath got all your brother Cokes his things, and help'd you to your beating, and the stocks; if you have a mind to hang him now, and show him your magistrate's wit, you may: but I should think it were better, recovering the goods, and to save your estimation in him. I thank you sir for the gift of your ward, Mistress Grace: look you, here is your hand and seal, by the way. Master Winwife, give you joy, you are Palemon, you are possess'd o' the gentlewoman, but she must pay me value, here's warrant for it. And honest madman, there's thy gown, and cap again; I thank thee for my wife. (*To the widow.*) Nay, I can be mad, sweetheart, when I please, still; never fear me. And careful Numps, where's he? I thank him for my license.

WASP.

How! Wasp *misseth the license.*

QUARLOUS.

'Tis true, Numps.

WASP.

I'll be hang'd then.

QUARLOUS.

Look i' your box, Numps. [*To* Justice.] Nay, sir, stand not you fix'd here, like a stake in Finsbury to be shot at, or the whipping post i' the Fair, but get your wife out o' the air, it will make her worse else; and remember you are but Adam, flesh and blood! You have your frailty, forget your other name of Overdo, and invite us all to supper. There you and I will compare our discoveries; and drown the memory of all enormity in your biggest

---

83. *estimation*] repute.

96. *Finsbury*] a public field outside London where archers practiced (Stow, I, 104).

bowl at home.

COKES.

How now, Numps, ha' you lost it? I warrant, 'twas when thou wert i' the stocks: why dost not speak?

WASP.

I will never speak while I live, again, for ought I know.

JUSTICE OVERDO.

Nay, Humphrey, if I be patient, you must be so too; this pleasant conceited gentleman hath wrought upon my judgment, and prevail'd: I pray you take care of your sick friend, Mistress Alice, and my good friends all—

QUARLOUS.

And no enormities.

JUSTICE OVERDO.

I invite you home with me to my house, to supper: I will have none fear to go along, for my intents are *ad correctionem, non ad destructionem; ad aedificandum, non ad diruendum:* so lead on.

COKES.

Yes, and bring the actors along, we'll ha' the rest o' the play at home. [*Exeunt.*]

The end.

---

110. *Mistress Alice*] Mrs. Overdo, not Punk Alice (cf. III.iii.11).

113–115. *ad . . . diruendum*] "for correction, not destruction, building up, not tearing down."

THE EPILOGUE.

Your Majesty hath seen the play, and you
  Can best allow it from your ear, and view.
You know the scope of writers, and what store
  Of leave is given them, if they take not more,
And turn it into license: you can tell
  If we have us'd that leave you gave us, well:
Or whether we to rage, or license break,
  Or be profane, or make profane men speak?
This is your power to judge, great sir, and not
  The envy of a few. Which if we have got,
We value less what their dislike can bring,
  If it so happy be, t' have pleas'd the King.

3–5. *what . . . license*] cf. Horace *Ars Poetica* 51.

Appendix

Chronology

	Political and Literary Events	Life and Works of Ben Jonson
1558	Accession of Queen Elizabeth. Thomas Kyd born. Robert Greene born.	
1560	George Chapman born.	
1561	Francis Bacon born.	
1564	Shakespeare born. Christopher Marlowe born.	
1570	Thomas Heywood born.*	
1572	Thomas Dekker born.* John Donne born. Massacre of St. Bartholomew's Day.	
1573		Benjamin Jonson born in London, June 11, 1573.*
1576	The Theatre, the first permanent public theater in London, established by James Burbage. John Marston born.	
1577	The Curtain theater opened. Holinshed's *Chronicles of England,*	

*Indicates that the year is approximate.

Scotland and Ireland.
Drake begins circumnavigation of the earth; completed 1580.

1579
John Fletcher born.
John Lyly's *Euphues: The Anatomy of Wit.*

1580
Thomas Middleton born.

1583
Philip Massinger born.

1584
Francis Beaumont born.*

1586
Death of Sir Philip Sidney.
John Ford born.

1587
The Rose theater opened by Henslowe.
Marlowe's *TAMBURLAINE* Part I.*
Greene's *ALPHONSUS KING OF ARAGON.**
Execution of Mary, Queen of Scots.

1588
Defeat of the Spanish Armada.
Marlowe's *TAMBURLAINE*, Part II.*

Leaves Westminster School; apprenticed as bricklayer.*

1589
Marlowe's *THE JEW OF MALTA.**
Greene's *FRIAR BACON AND FRIAR BUNGAY.**
Kyd's *THE SPANISH TRAGEDY.**

1590
Spenser's *Faerie Queene* (Books I–III) published.
Sidney's *Arcadia* published.
Shakespeare's *HENRY VI,* Parts

*Indicates that the year is approximate.

I–III,* *TITUS ANDRONICUS.**
Greene's *GEORGE-A-GREENE.*(?)*

1591

Shakespeare's *RICHARD III.**
Greene's *ORLANDO FURIOSO,** *JAMES THE FOURTH.**

1591–1592

Serves as a soldier in the Low Countries.*

1592

Marlowe's *DOCTOR FAUSTUS** and *EDWARD II.**
Shakespeare's *TAMING OF THE SHREW** and *THE COMEDY OF ERRORS.**
Death of Robert Greene.

1593

Shakespeare's *LOVE'S LABOUR'S LOST;** *Venus and Adonis* published.
Death of Marlowe.
Theaters closed on account of plague.

1594

Shakespeare's *TWO GENTLEMEN OF VERONA;** *The Rape of Lucrece* published.
Shakespeare's company becomes Lord Chamberlain's Men.
James Shirley born.*
Death of Kyd.

Marries Anne Lewis.

1595

The Swan theater built.
Sidney's *Defense of Poesy* published.
Shakespeare's *ROMEO AND JULIET,** *A MIDSUMMER NIGHT'S DREAM,** *RICHARD II.**

*Indicates that the year is approximate.
(?)Indicates that occurrence is in doubt.

Raleigh's first expedition to Guiana.

1596

Spenser's *Faerie Queene* (Books IV–VI) published.

Shakespeare's *MERCHANT OF VENICE,* KING JOHN.**

1597

Bacon's *Essays* (first edition).

Shakespeare's *HENRY IV,* Part I.*

Imprisoned for part authorship of a lost play, *THE ISLE OF DOGS.*

1598

Demolition of the Theatre.

Shakespeare's *MUCH ADO ABOUT NOTHING,* HENRY IV,* Part II.*

THE CASE IS ALTERED (Children of Chapel Royal).

Seven books of Chapman's translation of Homer's *Iliad* published.

EVERY MAN IN HIS HUMOR (Lord Chamberlain's Men).

Kills Gabriel Spencer, a fellow actor, in a duel; imprisoned but freed on plea of benefit of clergy; converted to Roman Catholicism while in jail.

1599

The Globe theater opened.

Shakespeare's *AS YOU LIKE IT,* HENRY V,* JULIUS CAESAR.**

Dekker's *THE SHOEMAKERS' HOLIDAY.**

Death of Spenser.

EVERY MAN OUT OF HIS HUMOR (Lord Chamberlain's Men).

1600

Shakespeare's *TWELFTH NIGHT,* HAMLET.**

Marston's *ANTONIO AND MELLIDA,* ANTONIO'S REVENGE.**

The Fortune theater built by Alleyn.

CYNTHIA'S REVELS (Children of Chapel Royal).

1601

Shakespeare's *MERRY WIVES OF WINDSOR.**

POETASTER (Children of Chapel Royal).

*Indicates that the year is approximate.

Insurrection and execution of the Earl of Essex.

1602

Shakespeare's *TROILUS AND CRESSIDA,** *ALL'S WELL THAT ENDS WELL.**

1603

Death of Queen Elizabeth; accession of James VI of Scotland as James I.
Florio's translation of Montaigne's *Essays* published.
Heywood's *A WOMAN KILLED WITH KINDNESS.*
Marston's *THE MALCONTENT.**
Shakespeare's company becomes the King's Men.

SEJANUS (King's Men).
Son Benjamin dies, aged 6.

1604

Shakespeare's *MEASURE FOR MEASURE,** *OTHELLO.**
Marston's *THE FAWN.**
Chapman's *BUSSY D'AMBOIS.**

1605

Shakespeare's *KING LEAR.**
Marston's *THE DUTCH COURTEZAN.**
Bacon's *Advancement of Learning* published.
The Gunpowder Plot.

Early masque at court, *THE MASQUE OF BLACKNESS.*
EASTWARD HO, in collaboration with Chapman and Marston (Children of the Queen's Revels); Jonson and Chapman imprisoned because of alleged derogatory allusions to King James.

1606

Shakespeare's *MACBETH.**
Tourneur's *REVENGER'S TRAGEDY.**
The Red Bull theater built.

VOLPONE (King's Men).

1607

Shakespeare's *ANTONY AND CLEOPATRA.**
Beaumont's *KNIGHT OF THE*

*Indicates that the year is approximate.

*BURNING PESTLE.**
Settlement of Jamestown, Virginia.

1608
Shakespeare's *CORIOLANUS,** *TIMON OF ATHENS,** *PERICLES.**
Chapman's *CONSPIRACY AND TRAGEDY OF CHARLES, DUKE OF BYRON.**
Richard Burbage leases Blackfriars Theatre for King's Company.
John Milton born.

1609
Shakespeare's *CYMBELINE;** *Sonnets* published.

EPICOENE (Children of the Queen's Revels).

1610
Chapman's *REVENGE OF BUSSY D'AMBOIS.**

THE ALCHEMIST (King's Men).
Returns to Anglican religion.*

1611
Authorized (King James) Version of the Bible published.
Shakespeare's *THE WINTER'S TALE,** *THE TEMPEST.**
Beaumont and Fletcher's *A KING AND NO KING.*
Tourneur's *ATHEIST'S TRAGEDY.**

CATILINE (King's Men).

1612
Webster's *THE WHITE DEVIL.**

1612–1613

Travels in France as tutor to son of Sir Walter Raleigh.

1613
The Globe theater burned.
Shakespeare's *HENRY VIII* (with Fletcher).
Webster's *THE DUCHESS OF MALFI.**
Middleton's *A CHASTE MAID IN CHEAPSIDE.*

*Indicates that the year is approximate.

1614
The Globe theater rebuilt.
The Hope theater built.

BARTHOLOMEW FAIR (Lady Elizabeth's Men).

1616
Death of Shakespeare
Death of Beaumont.

THE DEVIL IS AN ASS (King's Men).
Publication of Folio edition of *Works.*
Receives royal pension.

1618
Outbreak of Thirty Years War.
Execution of Raleigh.

1618–1619

Journeys on foot to Scotland; visits there with William Drummond.

1619

Given honorary M.A. by Oxford University.

1620
Pilgrim Fathers land at Plymouth.

1621
Middleton's *WOMEN BEWARE WOMEN.**

1622
Middleton's and Rowley's *THE CHANGELING.**

1623
Publication of Folio edition of Shakespeare's *COMEDIES, HISTORIES, AND TRAGEDIES.*

Lectures on rhetoric at Gresham College in London.(?)
Books and manuscripts lost when lodgings burn.

1625
Death of King James I; accession of Charles I.
Death of Fletcher.

1626
Death of Tourneur.

THE STAPLE OF NEWS (King's Men).

*Indicates that the year is approximate.
(?)Indicates that occurrence is in doubt.

Year		
1627	Death of Middleton.	
1628	Ford's *THE LOVER'S MELANCHOLY.*	Paralyzed by a stroke. Appointed chronologer of the City of London.
1629		*THE NEW INN* (King's Men).
1631	Shirley's *THE TRAITOR.* Death of Donne.	
1632	Death of Dekker.*	*THE MAGNETIC LADY* (King's Men).
1633	Donne's *Poems* published. Massinger's *THE CITY MADAM.**	*A TALE OF A TUB,* revised from an earlier play (Queen Henrietta's Men).
1634	Death of Chapman, Marston, Webster.*	A final "entertainment," *LOVE'S WELCOME AT BOLSOVER.*
1637		Jonson dies in Westminster, August 6; buried in Westminster Abbey, August 9.
1640	Death of Massinger.	
1640–1641		*Works* published, two volumes, folio, by Sir Kenelm Digby.
1641	Death of Heywood.	
1642	Shirley's *THE COURT SECRET* All theaters closed by Act of Parliament.	

*Indicates that the year is approximate.